PERSUADE
ON PURPOSE

CREATE PRESENTATIONS THAT INFLUENCE & ENGAGE

ERIC FITZPATRICK

IRISH   IRISH STORY

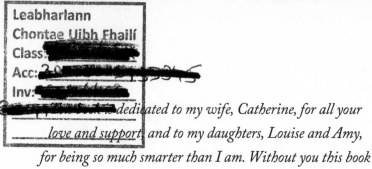
dedicated to my wife, Catherine, for all your love and support and to my daughters, Louise and Amy, for being so much smarter than I am. Without you this book would not exist.

MERCIER PRESS

Cork

www.mercierpress.ie

© Eric Fitzpatrick, 2017

ISBN: 978 1 78117 474 6

10 9 8 7 6 5 4 3 2 1

A CIP record for this title is available from the British Library

Printed and bound in the EU.

CONTENTS

INTRODUCTION

In December 2003 I was in Warrington in the north-west of England to deliver two presentations to the management team of Weldspares-Oki, the company for which I was working. When I finished the first one and sat back down, a colleague nudged me and said, 'Well done, Shergar.'

I asked him, 'What do you mean?' Shergar was a famous racehorse in the 1980s so I thought he was going to say that I had raced through my presentation. Instead he explained, 'All through your presentation, you were counting like a horse.' When trained to do so, horses count by pawing the ground in front of them in an exaggerated manner. During my presentation, I had tapped the floor with my foot in the same way that a horse counts, betraying my nerves.

That afternoon, as I stood to give my second presentation, the first thought that went through my head was, 'Don't move your feet.' I was halfway through the presentation (my feet hadn't moved!) when the pen I was holding, a cheap biro, snapped in two (I had been transferring it between my hands throughout the presentation and was holding it in both hands when it snapped). A tiny shard of plastic shot across the room and hit one of my colleagues on the side of the face.

If there's ever a moment that makes you realise you need to become better at delivering presentations, hitting someone in the face with a shard of plastic is it. So, in the spring of 2004 I joined Toastmasters International, an organisation founded in the 1920s by Ralph C. Smedley to help business people deal with their fear of speaking in public. Today it comprises more the 300,000 members in 13,000 clubs around the world. Then I started to study the techniques of speaking and presentation experts like Nancy Duarte, Garr Reynolds, Patricia Fripp, Jerry Weissman, Bill Gove, Brian Tracy, Dale Carnegie, and Dan and Chip Heath. I learned from winners of the World Championship of Public Speaking, like Jim Key, Darren LaCroix, Mark Brown, Ed Tate, Mark Hunter, Craig Valentine and David Brooks. I read their books, bought their CDs and DVDs, attended their seminars, and in recent years have even brought a couple of them to Ireland to deliver workshops to Toastmasters' members and the general public. Throughout this time I started giving as many presentations and speeches as possible. In the last ten years I have given more than 700 speeches or presentations in America, the UK and throughout Ireland, while working for Weldspares-Oki and more recently, since I set up my own business in 2009. The audiences have been as small as five and as large as 1,000.

What I have learned, during nearly ten years of study and practice, is that there are elements that go into presentations which make them memorable and engaging and persuade audiences to buy into your ideas – I call these 'positive score elements' – and there are elements which are used in presentations that make them dull and boring and cause audiences to lose interest – I call these 'negative score elements'. Once I had identified these elements, I decided to bring them together in such a way that speakers and presenters could use them to create as effective a presentation as possible. To that end I developed the 'Presentation Scorecard', a list of over eighty different elements found in presentations. It gives each element a score that reflects how effectively it helps or hinders a presentation. The idea is that the higher the score a presentation gets on the Presentation Scorecard, the more effective it will be.

The purpose of this book is to demonstrate how to use the Presentation Scorecard to consistently produce presentations of high quality and persuade audiences and prospective clients to buy into your ideas. The scorecard gives you a tangible way to measure the quality of your presentations. Think of it as being like a recipe for a cake. Your cupboard may hold an array of ingredients but only the exact quantity of the right ingredients mixed together in the correct way will result in a cake that is palatable. Likewise only the correct elements as outlined in the presentation scorecard and mixed in the right quantities will produce a palatable presentation.

Each chapter of the book concentrates on a different section of the Presentation Scorecard. It focuses on the elements relevant to that section, explains why an element helps (positive score element) or hinders (negative score element) a presentation and then sets out the score each element receives on the scorecard. Chapter 14 brings it all together and builds a presentation from scratch.

So how should you use this book? I suggest that you read it from cover to cover the first time. It will be tempting to go to a particular chapter that attracts your attention, but please resist. As I will highlight later on, many presenters actually begin to create a presentation from the wrong starting point. Don't do the same thing with this book. Take plenty of notes as you read. You will find ideas that appeal to you and ideas with which you disagree. Once you have read it the first time and have a clear understanding of the order in which a presentation should be created, then the book will become a reference guide, a resource to draw from every time you are creating a presentation.

The Presentation Scorecard really works. Using it, I have helped experienced presenters from large corporate clients win more sales by identifying the changes required to make their presentations more memorable, engaging and persuasive. In one case, the changes we implemented improved the presentation's score on the Presentation Scorecard by 910 points. In another it helped a client win a contract worth €1,000,000.

While the ideas I share in this book are focused on presentations, they are equally effective when giving speeches, pitching ideas, for one-to-one meetings and communicating in general.

I hope you enjoy it.

1

WHAT A TYPICAL PRESENTATION LOOKS LIKE

Before starting into the Presentation Scorecard, it is worth taking a look at the common problems of typical presentations, the type that most of us have attended at some time in our lives, the ones that have left us feeling less than inspired. Whenever I ask people what they think makes for a poor presentation, I tend to get the same responses: the presentation was hard to follow; it had no clear structure; the slides had too much text or were too technical; the presenter's delivery was lifeless; too much industry jargon was used; the presenter mumbled and was difficult to hear, or they spoke too fast; the presentation was too long, or it was boring. Unfortunately, the vast majority of presentations delivered today fall into many and sometimes all of these traps. So let's look at why this happens and the steps that can be taken to avoid making the same mistakes again.

WHY?

First let's look at why: why do presenters do these things? Why do they deliver presentations that they would complain about sitting through themselves? In fact, there are a number of reasons:

1. *Most people delivering professional presentations are not professional presenters.*

In most companies those who make the presentations are sales professionals, marketing professionals, accounting professionals, company directors and team leaders, who, on occasion, are called upon to deliver a presentation. Giving presentations is often a very small part of what they do. Some professionals might deliver 100 presentations per year (about 5 per cent of their working time), while others might deliver one every three months or, in some cases, only one a year. As a result most professionals learn just enough about delivering presentations to get by. They settle for being able to get through the occasion and never learn the skills and techniques required to deliver great presentations.

2. *Many presentations are prepared at short notice.*

You can picture the scene. Your boss comes to you on a Wednesday afternoon and says, 'I need you to deliver a presentation to the board/the sales team/the client this coming Friday.' You only have a couple of days to pull everything together and that's not enough time to gather up all the content you require, put it into an easy-to-follow structure, practise your delivery until you are comfortable with the material and then edit it to make it better. As a result, presenters choose to limit the risk of messing up by sticking solely to their message and the required information. This results in a dry, fact-based presentation that bores an audience to death.

3. *Most presenters focus on themselves and not on their audience.*

For a variety of reasons, presenters often focus on themselves when delivering presentations. They are nervous and want to make sure they don't make mistakes, don't forget their words and don't do anything to look foolish or embarrass themselves in front of their audience. This results in the presenter, consciously or unconsciously, doing everything in their power to protect themselves. They take no risks and stick solely to the facts and figures. They use industry-specific language that they are comfortable and familiar with (even if their audience is not) because it acts as a shield that protects them.

4. *Many presentations are built from the wrong starting point – the PowerPoint slides.*

Presenters often think that the place to start when preparing a presentation is with their PowerPoint slides. They make a decision to use the slides as notes to help them through their presentation and prepare them first so that they can refer to them when practising and preparing. This usually results in a set of slides that look more like a document than a visual aid and does nothing to enhance the presentation for the audience. If it's going to look like a document then it should be treated as a document and given to your audience as a handout (at the end of your presentation). If everything that you are going to say is on the slide and your audience can read it for themselves, why do they need you to present it to them?

Sometimes the company prepares slides and tells their presenters (often sales professionals) that these are the slides they must work from. This makes it very difficult for the presenters to infuse their own personalities into the presentation and creates a discord between the presenter, the slides and the audience.

WHAT?

Now that we know why presenters deliver poor presentations, the question that needs to be asked is what can you do to make presentations more effective? Even before we start looking at the Presentation Scorecard, the immediate way to improve any presentation you give is to stop doing the things that have just been discussed. Let's take a quick look at how you can do this.

1. *Most people delivering professional presentations are not professional presenters.*

The quickest way to improve your technique and make yourself a more professional presenter is to give presentations more often. Find opportunities outside your work environment to practise giving presentations. (Toastmasters International is one place you can do this.) Learn the skills and techniques required to be a great presenter. The key is to learn them when you don't need them so that you'll be comfortable using them when you do.

2. *Many presentations are prepared at short notice.*

There is not really much can be done about this – there will always be times when a presentation has to be prepared and delivered at short notice. The only way to deal with this is to become comfortable and familiar with the skills and techniques needed to make a good presentation (see point 1). If you do this it will be easier to pull together effective presentations at short notice.

3. Most presenters focus on themselves and not on their audience.

It's understandable that, as a presenter, you should think about your own well-being. After all, you're the person standing in front of the audience. You're the person who has set yourself up (or been set up) for a fall if the presentation goes badly. Moreover, standing on a platform with hundreds or thousands of pairs of eyes on you can be incredibly daunting. The secret to overcoming this is to realise that the presentation you are giving is not for you. You need to stop focusing on yourself and start focusing on your audience. When your audience becomes your focus you stop worrying about being perfect or screwing up. This helps you to relax, which helps you to deliver better presentations.

Remember, you are not, nor should you be, the centre of attention. Your presentation is about giving your audience useful information that can improve their situation, personally or professionally. The moment you realise this is the moment that some of the pressure you put on yourself is removed. You realise that you don't have to be perfect, that it's okay to have the odd stumble over your words and that some crutch words (often called 'filler words', these include 'ah', 'erm', 'you know', 'like' and 'so') are fine as long as they are not a distraction.

It's also OK to be nervous when giving a presentation. I still get nervous – the nerves never go away completely, nor should they. But if you concentrate on delivering the best presentation you can for the audience, then the nerves don't matter.

It's worth sharing here an experience I had myself, which helped me come to this realisation. In April 2010 I was due to give a speech to a group of 400 people. I'd never spoken to them before, so, wanting to make the speech as successful as possible, I rang a friend of mine, Paul, who had spoken to this group previously. I asked for his advice. He said, 'Listen, Eric, they're a great bunch. They'll be very supportive so just go and enjoy yourself.' Then he added, 'Remember this, as you're walking up onto the stage – I will be lying butt-naked on a hammock on a beach somewhere in Italy.' As soon as he said it, I started laughing, but I remember thinking at the time that that wasn't the advice I was looking for.

On the morning of the speech I was nervous, but did my best to keep calm. Ten minutes before I was due to speak I was still nervous. Nine, eight, seven, six minutes before, and I was still nervous. Five minutes before I was due to speak, this image of a butt-naked guy lying on a hammock on a beach somewhere in Italy popped into my brain and I started laughing. With that my level of nervousness dropped significantly and allowed my thinking to switch from myself to my audience. I walked onto the stage thinking, 'Just do the best you can for them.' I have never looked back. Up to that moment I had been creating presentations from a place of fear and had always taken myself too seriously. That moment removed most of the fear and allowed me to put what I was doing into context. It allowed me to realise that speeches and presentations are for audiences and not for the presenter.

4. Many presentations are built from the wrong starting point – the PowerPoint slides.

You need to stop building your presentations around PowerPoint slides and start building them around a clear objective (when thinking about what your objective is for your presentation, ask yourself what you are aiming to achieve). This objective should be focused on your audience and their needs. The PowerPoint slides should be the last piece of your presentation jigsaw, not the first. My rule of thumb is that you should create a presentation that could be delivered without PowerPoint slides, but would be enhanced, for the benefit of the audience, by any slides you use. The slides can then be created to support and complement the presentation.

These four issues are some of the most common reasons why presentations are dull, boring and lifeless, and I have outlined the most basic ways that they can be combated. What the Presentation Scorecard will do is show you in more detail what you need to do to create presentations that are memorable, engaging and persuasive and that audiences will want to listen to. It will show you how to change your thinking so that you will be able to create and deliver presentations that connect with your audience every time.

2

THE
PRESENTATION SCORECARD
(HOW IT WORKS)

In this chapter we will look at the basic layout of the Presentation Scorecard and I will provide a general explanation as to how it works. There are four components to the scorecard:

- The *eight key components* of great presentations.

- The *eighty-eight elements* found in presentations.

- The *four TRUE criteria* essential for great presentations.

- The *presentation template*.

The Presentation Scorecard is designed to be very easy to follow. It lists the different presentation components, the elements within each component, the score each element receives and each of the TRUE criteria it meets. It also leaves you room to score your own presentation.

Let's look now at the four components of the scorecard.

THE EIGHT PRESENTATION COMPONENTS
The scorecard is divided into eight essential components which, when you dissect your presentation into its component parts, are the sections that should be clearly visible:

1. The Pre-Presentation

2. The Presentation Opening

3. The Presentation Roadmap

4. The Presentation Message

5. Audience Engagement

6. The Presentation Delivery

7. The Presentation Close

8. The PowerPoint Slides

Each of these components will be looked at in detail in the following chapters.

Remember, presentations don't have to include PowerPoint slides, but I have included them here as a component part because of the frequency with which they are used. However, in many ways they have become a crutch for presenters, and it is important that you don't fall into this trap – they should only be used if they will enhance your presentation.

THE EIGHTY-EIGHT SCORECARD ELEMENTS

Each presentation component contains elements that will either help or hinder a presentation. Within the scorecard there are eighty-eight of these elements. The scoring system is straightforward. An element receives ten points for each of the TRUE criteria it meets (see below). Therefore, the maximum score each element can get is forty points. For example, an element such as a quotation will engage your audience and make them think, but won't necessarily help them to recall your message or make the message easier to understand. Therefore, a quotation will score twenty points. However, another element, a story, will make the audience think, will make it easier for them to recall the message, will make it easier for them to understand the message and will engage them. For that reason a story is an example of an element that scores the maximum forty points.

Where an element hinders the effectiveness of a presentation it is given a -40 score. An element with a minus score is deemed to meet none of the TRUE criteria and will in fact make it more difficult for the TRUE criteria to be met. An example of an element with a minus score is a PowerPoint slide that is full of text. The chapter on slides will explain this further.

In principle, the higher the score your presentation gets on the scorecard the more effective it will be. That said, you don't need to use every positive score element in each section every time. The idea is to recognise which elements will help your presentation and which ones will hinder it, and use the helpful ones accordingly.

THE FOUR TRUE CRITERIA

Great presentations need to meet four essential criteria. Meeting these criteria is what will help you to create and deliver a clear compelling message. Within each of the eight presentation components you will find elements that meet some or all of these criteria. The four TRUE criteria are:

1. **THINK**. Your presentation should make the audience think. They should be moved to consider the points or message you are making. Do they agree or disagree? To get them thinking, your message must be relevant to them and should offer them a new or alternative view.

2. **REMEMBER**. A great presentation should be easy to remember. The audience should be able to recall the key points and overriding message a day, a week, a month after the presentation has been delivered. Given that presentations are often delivered to influencers and not to the economic buyers or decision makers, it is important that influencers can recall your key points when they sit down with the economic buyer, which can be weeks after your presentation.

3. **UNDERSTAND**. A great presentation should be easy to understand. There should be no confusion or doubt. It should be easy to follow. It should have a logical sequence.

4. **ENGAGE**. A great presentation should engage the audience. It should grab their attention at the beginning and hold it throughout.

These are the criteria which are essential for the scoring of the elements of each of the eight components. I use the acronym TRUE to refer to these throughout the book.

THE PRESENTATION TEMPLATE

Finally there is the Presentation Template, which allows you to bring your presentation together quickly and effectively. Once you are familiar with the scorecard you can use the template to select the elements you want to include in your presentation. The difference between the Presentation Template and the scorecard itself is that the template only includes the elements that will help make your presentation as effective as possible.

HOW THE SCORECARD WILL HELP YOU

The Presentation Scorecard serves four purposes:

1. It lists the different elements that go into presentations and acts as a resource that can be drawn from every time you are creating a presentation. It should be close to hand whenever you are creating a new presentation or looking to improve an existing one. It will act as a reminder of the elements required and how they can help.

2. It provides a scoring system that allows you to measure the effectiveness of your presentation.

3. It helps speakers and presenters identify the changes required to improve an existing presentation. It will allow you to identify and remove the elements that could be having a negative impact on that presentation. It will also allow you to identify elements that could be used in a tangible way to improve the effectiveness and quality of the presentation.

4.   It can be used to set a minimum standard for all your presentations. It will help you to set the standard that works
for you. You simply select the elements that will make that
happen and leave out the ones that will hinder it.

However, at this point, I must add a few words of caution. For
any element on the scorecard to be of benefit to the presentation
and the audience, its content must be relevant to the presentation. Your presentation will not benefit from a story, a quotation
or any of the other positive score elements if the information
given does not relate to the message.

It is also possible that you will choose to include elements
in your presentation that are not listed on the Presentation
Scorecard. If you do so, then be sure to test them against the
TRUE criteria to measure the impact they will have on your
presentation.

Finally, the perception of what constitutes an acceptable
presentation today typically includes some of the elements
that you will find score in the negative on the scorecard. The
fact is, in my experience I have found that these elements
actually hinder the effectiveness of a presentation. They cause
audiences to stop listening and to start thinking about other
aspects of their life rather than focusing on the presentation.
They make presentations less memorable and harder to follow.
The reason I have included them in the scorecard is so you will
recognise them as elements to avoid in spite of their perceived
acceptability or current popularity. Examples of negative score
elements include slides with too much text, a presenter who

begins their presentation with a long-winded introduction about themselves and their organisation, and a presenter who finishes their presentation with a slide saying 'Thank You'.

When I put a typical presentation through the Presentation Scorecard its reliance on the negative elements means it often ends up with a minus score. Fortunately, it doesn't take too much work to identify and implement the changes required to increase the presentation's score. In one case, the changes I implemented resulted in a change of score from −320 to +590. The benefit to that client was a more memorable, engaging and persuasive presentation that helped win more sales.

Now, let's look in more detail at each of the eight presentation components and examine how you too can move your presentations from the negative to the positive. At the end of each chapter about the eight components, I have included the relevant part of the scorecard as a useful visual aid to quickly remind you of the elements you should be aiming for in each section.

3

THE PRE-PRESENTATION

As already discussed, when creating presentations most people start with slides and, in particular, slides that were used for a previous presentation. They don't realise that every presentation needs to be looked at in isolation and seen as a standalone event. While it can be perfectly acceptable to draw from slides that have been used previously, this should not be the starting point for creating a presentation. The slides should be the last part of the presentation puzzle.

So where should you start? The first thing that you must do when planning any presentation is to identify your objective.

IDENTIFYING YOUR OBJECTIVE

Start by asking yourself: what do I want to achieve with this presentation and what do I want my audience to do, think or believe at the end? Your presentation shouldn't simply be about what you say; it should also be about what your audience does afterwards.

One of the biggest mistakes I see sales organisations make is to deliver presentations that inform when they should be trying to persuade. I have sat through presentations delivered by sales professionals who were looking to win business from the company I represented, and all they talked about was their company, products and services. They shared information about when the company was formed, how many employees they had, what their annual turnover was. They supported this with an aerial view of the warehouse their products would be dispatched from if they won our business. This type of information has no value to a potential client. What they were doing was informing us who they were, when they would have been better served outlining the benefits that we would accrue from doing business with them. Telling us how we would make savings, increase revenue and enhance our company's reputation would have been of much greater interest.

TRUE Criteria (40 pts)

Clearly identifying the presentation objective in advance gives a presenter the best opportunity to meet the four TRUE criteria. A clear objective allows the presenter to use content that will contribute to the audience's thinking. It makes it easier for the presenter to engage with the audience and to present a straightforward message, making the presentation easier to understand and also to recall after the fact.

IDENTIFYING YOUR AUDIENCE

Once you have identified the objective of the presentation, the next thing to consider is the make-up of your audience, as this will affect the content you include in your presentation. Factors that will influence your content include age, gender, education, profession and company position. For example, the content of your presentation will differ when presenting to the board of a company as opposed to the staff of that same company. The board will be more interested in big-picture information, such as making savings, increasing revenue and strategic alliances. The staff will be more interested in the day-to-day logistics of the working relationship. They will be interested in knowing how a product works or gives them a competitive advantage over their competition. If, however, you were to start telling the board how a product works or what time deliveries would be made each day, they would lose interest very quickly.

Answering the question of who the audience is allows you to tailor the content to meet the specific needs of your audience and also to change your language to make it more appealing to each audience. An added advantage of answering this question is that a presenter shifts their thinking from themselves to their audience. This removes some of the self-inflicted pressure we apply to our presentations.

TRUE Criteria (40 pts)

Knowing and understanding your audience meets the four TRUE criteria.

BRAINSTORM

The next step in the pre-presentation phase is to brainstorm. Brainstorming is a problem-solving technique that involves one or more individuals developing or suggesting ideas in order to help solve a specific problem or problems. In the case of presentations, brainstorming will help solve the problems of what the most suitable content is and of how to control the amount of content used so the presentation is not too long. Even if you are preparing a presentation on your own, brainstorming is a must.

As a presenter you are perceived as an expert. This means that you have more information available to you than you will be able to fit in to the allotted time. The challenge is to identify which information to include and which to leave out. Brainstorming in the pre-presentation stage allows a presenter to get every idea out of their head so they can see which ideas, thoughts and pieces of information will be most relevant and useful for each presentation. Personally, I like to use Post-it notes when brainstorming. I write one idea per note, stick them onto a flip chart or whiteboard, and then arrange them in order of relevance.

It is important to understand why brainstorming needs to be done in the pre-presentation stage. Many presenters include way too much information in their presentations and they do so for a number of reasons. As they are constructing the presentation they keep thinking of new pieces of information to add, and throw in everything that comes to mind. They believe that the more information they include the better their presentation will be. Yet nothing could be further from the truth. Your audience doesn't want all of your information. They only want the most relevant information. Brainstorming in advance allows you to compare information and identify the most relevant.

Another reason that many presenters include too much information is that they see it as a type of protective cover. Their thinking is that if they include everything in the presentation it will protect them from looking foolish, from getting asked awkward questions. But it is better to have an audience that asks questions than one that has stopped listening because you had too much to say. For the record, no audience has ever complained that a presentation was too short. On the other hand, have you ever sat through a presentation that just went on and on and on and on and on? Don't make the same mistake!

TRUE Criteria (40 pts)

Brainstorming in the pre-presentation phase meets the four TRUE criteria.

CHOOSE A ROADMAP

The final essential step in the pre-presentation phase is to choose your presentation structure or 'roadmap'. Choosing a specific or clearly identifiable structure makes it easier for the presenter to plot their way through the presentation. It also makes it easier for the audience to follow. The common understanding is that a presentation must have an opening, a middle and an end. Choosing a specific structure strengthens the impact of the 'middle'. It also influences the content you include. In Chapter 5, which is devoted to roadmaps, I will explain in detail how they work, and guide you in selecting the most suitable one for your presentations.

TRUE Criteria (30 pts)

Choosing the presentation roadmap or structure in the pre-presentation phase contributes to making the presentation easier to engage with, understand and recall. It does not, however, help influence thinking.

POWERPOINT SLIDES

A useful, but non-essential part of a presentation, PowerPoint slides, when used correctly, can be a wonderful addition. Unfortunately, most presenters don't use them correctly. They are typically used by presenters as their own personal notes to help them plot their way through a presentation, but this is a fatal mistake to make.

Often when I get asked to work with a client on an upcoming presentation, they already have their slides ready to go, but yet they aren't even clear about what they want to achieve with their presentation! When we drill into their objective it usually changes the content and makes some of the slides redundant.

So remember: don't start preparing for a presentation with the slides and, particularly, don't start a new presentation with the slides you used during a previous presentation. The creation of the slides should be left until your presentation is finalised and you have all the other presentation components absolutely right.

TRUE Criteria (-40 pts)

Presenters who begin creating presentations by constructing their slides run the real risk of failing to meet the four TRUE criteria. The danger is that, because the presentation has been constructed from the wrong starting point, it will not contribute to their audience's thinking, it will be difficult to understand or recall and it will not engage.

PRESENTATION SCORECARD			
Pre-Presentation	**Points**	**TRUE Criteria**	**My Score**
Set a clear objective (what is my objective?)	40	TRUE	
Who is my audience? How will they benefit?	40	TRUE	
Brainstorm	40	TRUE	
Choose a roadmap	30	RUE	
PowerPoint slides	-40		

4

THE PRESENTATION OPENING

What is the objective of a presentation opening? Whenever I ask that question at workshops I get many different answers, for instance: 'It's to introduce yourself to your audience'; 'It's to tell your audience what you are going to talk about'; 'It's to build rapport with your audience'. These are all good answers but not how I view it. In my opinion, the objective of a presentation opening is TO DISRUPT YOUR AUDIENCE'S THINKING.

When they come to hear your presentation, audience members have so many different things going on in their lives. As they wait to hear you speak, their thoughts could be on family, friends, work, emails or holidays, just to name a few things. Each is important to them and your job as a presenter is to find a way to say to the audience, 'Look, I know you have all of these other things going on in your life but, for the next twenty minutes, give me your undivided attention.' As a presenter, you might be thinking, 'If they have come to hear my presentation the least they can do is listen to me when I'm speaking.' However, it's not their job to stop thinking about the different aspects of their lives; it's the presenter's job to make them want to stop.

Think about the opening sequence to the James Bond movie *Skyfall*. It runs for eleven minutes and thirty-five seconds and its sole purpose is to get cinemagoers to leave all the other aspects of their lives at the cinema door and give Bond their undivided attention, before the main story of the movie starts. It worked for me. At the end of the opening sequence – when Bond gets shot and falls off the top of the train and into a ravine – the thought that went through my head was, 'Is he dead?', followed very quickly by, 'Ah Eric, you eejit. If he was dead that would be the end of the movie.' As an opening, however, it had achieved its purpose. The only thing going through my mind was what might have happened to Bond. Everything else of importance in my life had been pushed to one side. As presenters, that must be our aim at the beginning of our presentations.

In 1978 Hartley and Davies carried out a study, *Note Taking: A Critical Review*, which showed that audiences are at their most attentive at the beginning and end of a presentation.[1] That is why it is so important to get the presentation opening right. When your audience is at their most attentive, you better have something to say that they find worth listening to. If you don't then your audience will lose interest very quickly and switch off.

There are many ways to begin a presentation: some will help you get your message across and some will hinder it.

---

1 Hartley, J. and Davies, I. K., 'Note Taking: A Critical Review', *Innovations in Education and Training International*, vol. 15, no. 3, 1978, pp. 207–24.

OPENINGS THAT HINDER

Audiences want to receive valuable information and knowledge, and they want it delivered in a way that engages them. None of the following three types of openings will convey that you are capable of doing that.

Introductory opening

Often presenters will begin a presentation by introducing themselves to their audience: 'Hi, my name is Eric Fitzpatrick and my company is Ark Speaking and Training.' Presenters start with an opening like this because it is safe and cannot be challenged by the audience. However, in my experience, the only time this is appropriate is if you have never met your audience before and you haven't been introduced to them beforehand by someone else. For me, this is not a strong enough opening as it will not disrupt your audience's thinking. It is more about you than for your audience. Imagine your audience is going to say, 'So what?' to everything you say. 'Hi, my name is Eric Fitzpatrick.' 'So what?' 'My company is Ark Speaking and Training.' 'So what?' What your audience is saying is, 'What relevance does this have to me?'

Honestly, I wouldn't start with an introduction even in a situation where you don't know the audience and haven't been introduced to them. Instead, start with an opening that grabs their attention and then introduce yourself. One way to do this is to tell them a story or get them to do something. In one case I asked everyone in an audience of 120 to stand up, turn to the person next to them and say, 'Hi, you're my partner.' I then gave them an exercise to do as partners. Once they had completed it successfully, I showed them how they could have carried it out slightly differently and in doing so, produced a better result. This exercise worked for two reasons: first, it got everybody involved at the beginning of the presentation and second, it allowed me to reinforce one of the points I wanted the audience to take away from the presentation.

TRUE Criteria (-40 pts)

The introductory opening doesn't meet any of the four TRUE criteria. It doesn't influence the audience's thinking and, because it is not relevant to them, it does not contribute to helping them understand or recall your message. It also does nothing to engage them.

Apologetic opening

The second type of opening that hinders you in getting your message across is the apologetic opening. This is when the presenter starts by saying something like, 'Ladies and gentlemen, I haven't had much time to prepare for this presentation so please forgive me if I get a couple of things wrong or if the slides aren't perfect.' This opening is purely for the presenter. It is to protect themselves from looking foolish due to lack of care or preparation.

I know that sometimes a presenter is asked to deliver a presentation at short notice and has very little time to prepare, but even then this type of opening doesn't help or add value for your audience. Remember your audience doesn't know or care how much time you had to prepare or how much notice you were given in advance. They only care about how they can benefit from listening to your presentation. Starting off like this will not only fail to grab them, but it could lower their expectations and make them less inclined to listen than before.

TRUE Criteria (-40 pts)

Again this meets none of the four TRUE criteria.

Grateful opening

The third type of opening that will stop you gaining the audience's attention is the grateful opening. This is where the presenter starts by saying something like, 'Ladies and gentlemen, I would just like to start by saying thank you for giving me the opportunity to speak with you today', or 'Thanks for taking the time to let me make this presentation to you today.' As with the introductory opening, presenters use this type of opening because it is safe and they can protect themselves with it. Presenters believe that their audience will appreciate that the presenter is grateful for the opportunity to speak. However, if you have valuable knowledge to share with your audience, then it is they who should be grateful to you for taking the time to share it with them.

TRUE Criteria (-40 pts)

The same is true for the grateful opening as the apologetic opening. It meets none of the four TRUE criteria.

OPENINGS THAT HELP

A question

Questions grab our attention. They force us to consider them and our answer to them. When we do that, our thinking is disrupted. Questions bring audiences into the presentation, so it can be very beneficial to start a presentation by asking your audience a question. This gets them thinking about the subject (obviously the question must have a connection to the subject of the presentation). Questions make the audience active participants and that active participation is easier to remember a day or a week later, along with the message behind the presentation.

TRUE Criteria (20 pts)

Questions meet two of the TRUE criteria. They give audiences cause to think and at the moment that they are thinking about the question, or their answer to the question, they are engaged in the presentation.

A story

An even better alternative is to start with a story. Stories get audiences thinking, they are memorable and they make our message easier to remember. Stories generate understanding and they engage.

Have you ever listened to someone telling a story and found yourself completely engrossed in it? They are, in my opinion and the opinion of others, the single most powerful tool a presenter or speaker can have. Patricia Fripp, an internationally renowned speaking coach, has said: 'No one can resist a good story, well told.'[2]

For me, stories are so powerful that I am devoting a full chapter (Chapter 9) to them. For now let me just say that a well-told story at the beginning of a presentation will absolutely disrupt your audience's thinking and grab their attention.

TRUE Criteria (40 pts)

Stories meet the four TRUE criteria.

A quotation

A quotation that is attributed to someone else – particularly someone famous or an expert in the topic you are discussing – is a great way to grab an audience's attention. However, you must ensure that the quote is related to your message. The quotation can be one that is familiar to your audience, one that they have never heard before, or one that is controversial. Whichever it is, it must be attributed to the originator. If the origins of the quote are in dispute, you can start with, 'As someone once said …'. If the quote is controversial, then it is more effective to state the quote and then (after a slight pause) attribute it.

Whatever type of quote you use, it will capture your audience's attention, engage them and get them thinking. In the past I have delivered workshops on adding humour to presentations and have begun the workshop as follows: 'John Cleese once said, "If I can make you laugh, I can get you to like

---

2 Fripp P., 'How to Prepare and Present Powerful Persuasive Presentations', seminar, Dublin, October 2014.

me. If you like me you will be more open to my ideas."' I then explained that, in my opinion, this was one of the reasons why it was necessary to use humour in presentations. Starting with a quote that was directly relevant to the presentation drew the audience in and helped them to focus on the techniques I was there to share with them over the next few hours.

TRUE Criteria (20 pts)

A suitable or relevant quotation will meet two of the TRUE criteria. It will give audiences cause to think and at the moment that they are thinking about the quotation (even if they disagree with the quote) they are engaged in the presentation.

A challenge

Exactly as the name suggests, a challenge throws down a gauntlet to your audience. In essence, it offers a point of view with which your audience might not agree. It could be as simple as saying, 'Ladies and gentlemen, over the next twenty minutes I am going to demonstrate how Model B is a better product than the model you are currently using.' For example, given that mobile users are often fans of specific brands, it might sound something like, 'Ladies and gentlemen, over the next twenty minutes I am going to demonstrate why the Samsung S6 is a better phone for business than the Apple iPhone 6.' In a case like this, an iPhone user will give you their full attention because they want to prove you wrong. A challenge will certainly engage your audience and get them thinking. It can also help them to remember your presentation if your challenge connected with them emotionally. Maybe you made them angry at the thought of any phone being better than theirs.

TRUE Criteria (30 pts)

Laying down a challenge will meet three of the TRUE criteria. They give audiences cause to think and at the moment that they are thinking about the challenge they are engaged in the presentation. A challenge also aids recall when it connects on an emotional level.

An interesting statistic

Audiences are curious. They attend presentations looking to learn something new. A statistic that is new and relevant to them will grab their attention. Here are a couple of examples. Do you know what the chances are of becoming an astronaut? 1 in 13,200,000. What are the chances of getting struck by lightning? 1 in 576,000. Statistics like this engage audiences and make them think, but if you are going to use them, make sure they are relevant to the presentation message. They might, on some occasions, be the one thing that a member of your audience can remember after your presentation.

TRUE Criteria (20 pts)

Interesting statistics meet two of the TRUE criteria. They will give audiences cause to think and at the moment that they are thinking about the statistics, they are engaged in the presentation.

Reference what is on the mind of the audience

Sometimes the only way to begin a presentation is to reference something that is on the mind of the audience, particularly if it is something that could be a barrier between you and them.

For example, it could be the temperature of the room in which you are speaking: 'Ladies and gentlemen, just before I start, can I ask if everyone is warm enough? It's not too cold (or hot), is it?'

It could be the noise outside the room. 'Ladies and gentlemen, is the noise outside a distraction? Do you need to close a window or try to get the noise stopped before I start?'

It could be that the audience is very tired (at the end of a work day or a conference) and are ready to go home or head to their hotel. 'Ladies and Gentlemen, I know it's been a long day (or a long three days) so can we come to an agreement? I will cut my presentation short if, in return, you give me your undivided attention.'

It could be that you are speaking before lunchtime and your audience is hungry: 'Ladies and gentlemen, I know that you must be hungry at this stage and I am the only thing keeping you from lunch, so here's my promise to you. Give me your undivided attention for the next twenty minutes and I will finish early so you can get to lunch a little early.'

It could be a reference to something within the company or business that everyone is aware of (poor sales figures, competitor activities, company takeover): 'Ladies and gentlemen, I'm sure you are all wondering how we are going to address the poor sales figures we achieved last year. Over the next twenty minutes I will show you the plan we have to turn around our fortunes.'

This opening engages an audience because it shows that you are aware of what they are thinking about and are not just focused on giving a presentation.

TRUE Criteria (10 pts)

Referencing something that is on the mind of the audience meets one of the TRUE criteria. It engages audiences because they recognise that you are thinking about them. In many cases it will not contribute to their thinking, aid understanding or recall, simply because what you reference is related directly to the audience, event or location, and has nothing to do with your message.

Reference something mentioned earlier

If your presentation is one of a number of presentations being delivered to an audience on the same day (for example, at a conference), making reference to something that resonated with the audience from a previous presentation can add impact to your own. A good presenter will recognise what they can use that will make this sort of connection. It might be a reference to something that made them laugh, surprised them or got them thinking. By doing this, you will engage your audience, because it shows that, like them, you are tuned in to the events of the day and not just delivering a canned presentation. This creates a connection between presenter and audience.

TRUE Criteria (10 pts)

Referencing something mentioned earlier meets one of the TRUE criteria. It engages the audience because they are familiar with what you are referencing, although it does not meet the other TRUE criteria as it will probably not be directly linked to your own presentation.

Humour

Humour is a very effective way to open a presentation. By humour, I do not mean a joke. Some presenters will start a presentation by telling a joke in the hope that it will generate laughter. In my opinion, you should not start with a joke. Jokes get told badly, are not usually as funny as the presenter thinks they are and run the risk of alienating an audience.

In contrast, humour used properly helps to build a connection between you and your audience. It disrupts their thinking and helps put them at ease, which will make them more open to listening to and buying into your message. In Chapter 8 I will share a number of ideas that can be used to generate humour at the beginning of and throughout your presentation.

TRUE Criteria (30 pts)

Humour meets three of the TRUE criteria. It engages the audience and aids recall and understanding.

State your outcomes

Sometimes the best way to begin a presentation is to state

upfront exactly what your audience can expect from your presentation. Importantly, the outcomes your audience can expect must be stated from their perspective. Don't tell them what you do; instead, tell them how they can benefit from what you do.

This type of opening works well when presenting to corporate-level executives, business owners and people who need big picture information rather than the finer details. It works because it gets your audience thinking about how they can apply your ideas, service or products to their business needs. It can sound something like this: 'Ladies and gentlemen, over the next twenty minutes I am going to demonstrate how our product/service can help you save/improve/grow, etc.' As part of an internal presentation to bosses or management it might sound like: 'Ladies and gentlemen, over the next twenty minutes I will demonstrate how we will reach our company targets over the next twelve months.'

TRUE Criteria (40 pts)

Stating your outcomes at the beginning of the presentation meets the four TRUE criteria. It has the ability to make audiences think about how your message can benefit or affect them. It will make your message easier to remember or recall because it has been stated at the outset. It makes the message easier to understand because it provides a reference for the remainder of the presentation and it engages your audience. If the outcomes you state at the beginning of your presentation are of benefit to your audience, then they will listen attentively because they will want to know more about how you can help them.

A scripted opening

I am a huge believer in writing out a speech or presentation word-for-word. Seeing the words in writing gives you a better perspective of their flow and structure in a way that isn't available through the spoken word. It's not always possible to write out a speech word-for-word because the presentation is too long or because the presentation has to be delivered at short notice. That said, there are two sections of the speech/presentation that I believe must be written out word-for-word: the opening and the close. As I said earlier, audiences are at their most attentive at the beginning and end of a presentation. These may be the only parts of your presentation that they can remember afterwards, so it makes sense to give yourself the best chance of saying exactly what you need them to hear.

There are two additional benefits to writing out the opening. First, the opening of a presentation is when a presenter is at their most nervous. This is where you are more likely to stumble over your words or speak too fast. Writing out the opening allows you to memorise exactly what you want your audience to hear and reduces your chances of forgetting vital points or information. Second, writing out your opening allows you to see where improvements can be made to the flow and sound of the words.

Some presenters believe that presentations should not be

written out. They think this inhibits a presenter's natural style and will make a presentation sound canned or rehearsed. This, in my opinion, is a cop out. Done correctly it can only enhance the impact of your presentation.

So how do you do it correctly? The written word is different from the spoken word so, for me, it is imperative to speak the words first and write/type those words out onto your page as you go. After this, you must be prepared to do as much rewriting as is necessary. The first draft will not be your best work, but, as you get into the process of redrafting your presentation, better ways of expressing the same idea will come to you. Ernest Hemingway once said: 'The first draft of anything is shit.' If rewriting worked for Hemingway, then it can certainly work for you.

Writing out your words also allows you to memorise and rehearse them. Repeated rehearsal cements the words in your memory and makes them easier to recall. When we have memorised the words, then we can practise delivering the lines so that they sound natural and unrehearsed. This is what actors do, and on stage or screen great actors make it seem effortless only after they have put in the work to get to that point. Presenters should be aiming to do the same.

Writing out your opening – as well as the rest of the speech, if possible – enables you to find the right words. Mark Twain once said: 'The difference between the almost right word and the right word is really a large matter – 'tis the difference between the lightning bug and the lightning.' Most presenters don't take the time to find the right word and make it part of the right sentence. Scripting your opening, however, gives you the chance to make the right sort of impact with your words and in a sales environment this gives you a vital advantage over your competition.

TRUE Criteria (30 pts)

Scripted openings meet three of the TRUE criteria. They have the ability to make audiences think about how your message can benefit or affect them. They can contribute to understanding because they give a presenter the chance to say what they need to say in the most effective way. They also engage. Carefully crafted words built around a relevant message and delivered with confidence are compelling to listen to.

THINK TRUE PRESENTATIONS

The objective of the presentation opening is to disrupt your audience's thinking. You now know how some of the common ways that presenters begin their presentations will actually hinder rather than increase the impact you are trying to have. However, there are many really effective ways to open a presentation. The key is to identify the ones that you are comfortable using and utilise them well. But whichever ones you choose to use, where possible, always script your opening and rehearse it word-for-word. Knowing your opening this well will help you when you are at your most nervous.

PRESENTATION SCORECARD			
Presentation Opening	**Points**	**TRUE Criteria**	**My Score**
Introductory opening	-40		
Apologetic opening	-40		
Grateful opening	-40		
A question	20	TE	
A story	40	TRUE	
A quotation	20	TE	
A challenge	30	TRE	
An interesting statistic	20	TE	
Reference what is on the mind of the audience	10	E	
Reference something mentioned earlier	10	E	
Humour	30	RUE	
State your outcomes	40	TRUE	
A scripted opening	30	TUE	

5

THE PRESENTATION ROADMAP OR STRUCTURE

Once you have decided on the type of opening you are going to use, it is then time to choose the structure to apply to the main part of your presentation to make it work most effectively. A good presentation structure will make a presentation easier to understand, will engage your audience and keep them thinking about the presentation's message.

The structure of a presentation is often seen as less important than the content or the delivery. Most presenters and speakers believe that a presentation or a speech should have an opening, a middle and an end, and tend to leave it at that. However, given that the purpose of a presentation is to provide knowledge, information or ideas that are of value to your audience, then as presenters we should do everything we can to make it as easy as possible for our audience to receive the knowledge, information or ideas. The right presentation structure or roadmap is essential in making your presentation easy to follow and understand. It allows your audience to focus on thinking about how your message will help them, instead of trying to work out what you are saying.

I am now going to share some presentation roadmaps that will help you to do that.

USEFUL TYPES OF ROADMAPS

The numerical roadmap

The numerical roadmap does exactly as the name suggests. The titles of these types of presentations are usually centred round a number of ideas, tips, reasons, etc. Sample titles include: '5 ways to grow your sales', '7 ideas that will make cold-calling easier', '10 presentation mistakes to avoid'.

This type of presentation is easy to follow and has the added benefit of allowing your audience to see the progress of your presentation. For example, if your presentation is entitled '5 ways to grow your sales', then your audience knows that you are halfway through the presentation when you get to the third way. Knowing this makes it easier for your audience to commit to the remainder of your presentation. If your audience doesn't know how long your presentation is going to be, you run the risk of having them become distracted, wondering how much longer the presentation will last. When this occurs, they are not thinking about what you want them thinking about, i.e. the message of the presentation.

TRUE Criteria (30 pts)

The numerical roadmap meets three of the TRUE criteria. It contributes to making your presentation easier to follow and understand. It keeps the audience engaged because it allows them to focus on the message, and because it is easy to understand it will be easier to recall.

The chronological roadmap

The chronological roadmap allows your audience to follow your presentation and presentation message along a timeline. It usually starts with the earliest date and works through relevant dates until you reach the most recent date. Using a chronological roadmap clarifies the order in which events took place. This works if you are explaining a sequence of events, giving the background to your company, or taking your audience through a new product from research to launch. A couple of years ago I helped a client with a presentation and they chose to use the chronological structure. They wanted to speak about the significant events in their business' life. They began by talking about the formation of the company in 1983 as a distributor. How, in 1985, it moved into manufacturing; how, in 1992, they established their first division in the United Kingdom. They then spoke about setting up a research and development facility in 2000, establishing a base in the Middle East in 2008 and how they celebrated thirty years in business in 2013.

In the case of your company you might start by stating the year the company was formed, then follow that with major events in the company's life, like when you expanded into a new market for the first time, or when you made your first acquisition, or reached a certain level of turnover, or employed a significant number of people.

TRUE Criteria (30 pts)

The chronological roadmap meets three of the TRUE criteria. It makes your presentation easier to follow and understand, and it keeps the audience engaged. Because it is easy to understand, it makes it easier to recall a day, a week or a month later.

The situation/solution roadmap

Again as the name suggests, the situation/solution roadmap starts out by explaining a current situation that a company might be experiencing and then offers a solution.

The situation in this scenario is usually negative. Companies use this roadmap when they have to explain to staff or shareholders where the company stands today and what they are going to do to rectify the situation. For example, if a company has had a bad year financially, this roadmap allows the presenter to clarify the current situation and explain what they are going to do to improve their financial fortunes. The solution might have a number of different aspects to it: introducing new products, expanding to new markets, making some staff redundant.

Furthermore, in a sales scenario, this roadmap might be used if a company has let down a client. This roadmap allows the client to understand that you recognise how they have been let down and what you are going to do to address the situation and hopefully ensure it doesn't happen again.

TRUE Criteria (40 pts)

The situation/solution roadmap meets the four TRUE criteria. It contributes to the audience's thinking, keeps them engaged and makes the presentation easy to understand and recall later.

The features/benefits roadmap

The features/benefits roadmap is often used by sales professionals to illustrate a product, service or idea. A presenter will use this structure to explain a specific feature of a product and then highlight the benefits of that feature. They will then talk about the next specific feature and explain its benefits. The important thing here is to explain the benefits in terms that are of interest to the audience. The benefit must be relevant to them.

Take Skechers footwear as an example. One of the most important things people look for when buying shoes is comfort. With the Skechers range, one of the most important features is that they are extremely lightweight, with the result that they are very comfortable. Therefore, if you were making a features/benefits presentation for Skechers, this is one of the features/benefits that you would use.

TRUE Criteria (40 pts)

The features/benefits roadmap meets the four TRUE criteria.

The rhetorical question roadmap

This is my favourite. The rhetorical question roadmap is a question and answer roadmap. It allows you to build your presentation around a series of questions that you believe your audience would want answers to and gives you the opportunity to provide those answers – for example, a typical question might be 'How do we plan to grow our business over the next twelve months?' – followed by an explanation of the actions or changes that are going to be implemented to grow the business over that period.

There are a number of benefits to this roadmap. It is very easy for the audience to follow as they hear the question and then the answer to that question. It is also a very useful roadmap if you find that the time allocated to your presentation has been reduced (this can happen at a conference) as the presenter can simply shorten their presentation by removing a question and its answer.

TRUE Criteria (40 pts)

The rhetorical question roadmap meets the four TRUE criteria.

The modular roadmap

A modular roadmap is made up of a number of sections, all of which are relevant to the message you want to get across in your presentation, but are still independent of each other. For example, a sales presentation might include a section on the features and benefits of products, a section on customer service, a section on marketing support and a section on competitors' activities. A company-focused presentation that uses this roadmap might talk about the different parts of the business: sales and marketing, the accounts department and financial control, warehouse dispatch and return, and finally their IT support capabilities. In both cases the different sections are relevant to the central message that the presenter is looking to deliver, while still being independent of each other. One benefit of this structure is that, if a presenter needed to make changes to a presentation in terms of content or length, they can change or remove one section without impacting on the rest of the presentation.

TRUE Criteria (30 pts)

The modular roadmap meets three of the TRUE criteria. It makes the content easier to understand and recall because of how the content is presented. It also contributes to keeping the audience engaged because they find this type of presentation easy to follow.

The compare and contrast roadmap

As the name suggests, this roadmap is used to describe two subjects, such as people, places, events, products etc. It offers both the similarities and the differences between the subjects and serves to illustrate why one might be might be preferable to the other.

TRUE Criteria (30 pts)

The compare and contrast roadmap meets three of the TRUE criteria in that it contributes to the audience's thinking and promotes both understanding and engagement.

The case study roadmap

A case study is defined as the analysis of people, events, decisions, projects or other systems that are studied by agreed methods over a period of time. In presentation terms, a case study roadmap would be used to present information based on that type of analysis. For example, if an organisation was launching a new product they might use a case study roadmap to explain the testing that was carried out on that product and the results that were generated. In a sales environment this type of roadmap would provide supporting evidence to a client or potential client about how they would benefit from using the new product. This roadmap may incorporate elements of other roadmaps, such as features/benefits or a chronological structure, but it differs in that it is focused solely on the one project, event, decision, group of people, etc.

TRUE Criteria (30 pts)

The case study roadmap meets three of the TRUE criteria. It aids understanding and recall because of how the content is presented, and keeps the audience engaged because they find this type of presentation easy to follow.

Background, research, methods, summary, Q&A roadmap

Sometimes you won't be able to use the roadmap of your choice. Some industries have a presentation roadmap that presenters are expected to follow. The scientific and medical fields expect presenters to follow the background, research, methods, summary and Q&A roadmap. While I don't usually agree with finishing on questions, I do acknowledge that it is required in certain circumstances. When scientists, researchers or the medical profession present new information, they expect to be challenged at the end of their presentation. They receive questions challenging their assertions or findings. This is the only time that I accept the need to finish on questions.

Where there is a clear expectation for you to follow a particular structure, it is best to do so. The danger with not following it is that your audience will focus on what you are not doing instead of the message you are trying to get across. The benefit of this lack of choice is that it is one less thing to have to think about.

TRUE Criteria (40 pts)

The background, research, methods, summary, Q&A roadmap meets the four TRUE criteria because it is the accepted roadmap for its industry or field. It keeps them thinking about your message, not the structure of the presentation. It makes the content easier to understand and recall because of how it is presented. It also contributes to keeping the audience engaged because they are familiar with this roadmap and find this type of presentation easy to follow.

THE OPENING, MIDDLE AND CLOSE

Roadmaps aside, all presentations must follow the traditional formula of having an opening, a middle and a close. As already stated, audiences benefit from having a structure that allows them to plot their way through your presentation and having these three clearly defined parts helps them to do so.

For me, the key to the opening, middle and close structure is how you transition from one section to the next. The clearer you can make this transition the better. The best way to do this is with phrases that clearly indicate that you are moving from one section to the next.

At the end of the opening section of a presentation, for example, I will state clearly what the audience can expect from the presentation. I use this to indicate that I am leaving the opening of my presentation and moving into the middle section. For example, having used an attention-disrupting opening such as a question, provocative statement or a quick and relevant story (see Chapter 4), I will then use a phrase such as, 'So ladies and gentlemen, over the next twenty minutes I am going to share with you five ideas for making presentations more effective and show you how you can apply them to your future presentations.' For the rhetorical question roadmap that might sound like, 'So ladies and gentlemen, the question is, why should you consider choosing us as your strategic partner for the next twelve months? In the next twenty minutes, I am going to outline five ways in which I believe partnering with us will be of benefit to you.'

A phrase like this works for a number of reasons. First, it tells the audience what you are going to be talking about, which brings clarity and understanding. Second, it gives an indication of the duration of the presentation. This helps to keep your audience engaged (audiences like to know how long a presentation will last). Perhaps most importantly, however, it is alerting the audience to the fact that you are about to move on to the main part of the presentation.

In her workshops and seminars, speaking coach Patricia Fripp refers to these as 'transition phrases'.[1] This is a phrase

---

1 Fripp P., 'How to Prepare and Present Powerful Persuasive Presentations', seminar, Dublin, October 2014.

that allows a presenter to move seamlessly from one part of their presentation to the next and which makes it easy for their audience to follow. In my opinion, this type of phrase should be followed by a pause. It is a natural point in a presentation for an audience to take stock of what the presenter has said so far and the pause gives them time to do so. The pause, in a way, should be part of the transition.

TRUE Criteria (20 pts)

A clear opening, middle and close meets two of the TRUE criteria. It contributes to making the presentation easier to understand and to recall later.

NO CLEAR STRUCTURE

Audiences switch off during presentations. No matter how good or engaging your presentation is there will be occasions when audience members become distracted and start thinking about the important things in their lives. Having no clear structure makes it harder for them to get back on track when they return.

The failure to choose a clear structure in advance for your presentation also means that you might unintentionally use a number of different roadmaps. You will potentially move from a numerical roadmap to a chronological map, then on to a rhetorical question, followed by elements of a features/benefits roadmap and finally return to the numerical or chronological structure. This confuses an audience and makes it more difficult for them to follow your presentation.

If an audience member has switched off when you were using a numerical roadmap and returns when you are using a chronological or rhetorical roadmap, they will find themselves wondering how you got to where you are in the presentation. Their thinking will be: 'The presenter was giving us five ways to do something and now they are taking us through the timeline of the organisation/product, etc. How did we get there? What have I missed?'

The audience member now has a choice. Carry on listening to the presenter and forget about what they might have missed; ignore what the presenter is saying and try to fill in the gap, thereby missing what you are saying at that point; or switch off permanently because it is too difficult to follow. Given these three choices, audiences will nearly always choose to switch off permanently.

TRUE Criteria (-40 pts)

The lack of a clear structure hinders audience engagement and understanding, makes it difficult to remember what you said and can stop them from thinking about your message.

HOW MANY STRUCTURES/ROADMAPS CAN YOU USE IN A SINGLE PRESENTATION?

One or two roadmaps in a single presentation is perfectly acceptable, if used intentionally. Any more than that and a presentation runs the risk of confusing your audience. The key is to *deliberately select roadmaps*. Equally, it is important to select roadmaps that you are comfortable with and to recognise that some roadmaps will suit certain presentations better than others.

PRESENTATION SCORECARD			
Body of Presentation	**Points**	**TRUE Criteria**	**My Score**
Numerical roadmap	30	RUE	
Chronological roadmap	30	RUE	
Situation/Solution roadmap	40	TRUE	
Feature/Benefit roadmap	40	TRUE	
Rhetorical Question roadmap	40	TRUE	
Modular roadmap	30	RUE	
Compare and Contrast roadmap	30	TUE	
Case Study roadmap	30	RUE	
Background, Research, Methods, Summary, Q&A roadmap	40	TRUE	
Opening, middle, close	20	RU	
No Clear Structure	- 40		

6

THE PRESENTATION MESSAGE

The purpose of a presentation is to deliver a message to the audience. The presenter gives them an idea, information or knowledge that they can start applying almost immediately and benefit from doing so. The message in a presentation is often different from the presentation objective. While a presenter's objective might be to persuade an audience to buy into their product or service, the message of the presentation might be that the particular product or service is the best quality, or represents the best value, or is the most competitively priced.

The following are some dos and don'ts when it comes to messages.

DOS

A clear message

A presenter's job is to deliver a message to their audience. The clearer the message is the better. The message mustn't be ambiguous. It can't mean different things to different people. This isn't always easy to get right. The best way to avoid ambiguity and make your message easy to understand and remember, is by keeping that message as simple as possible. Sometimes the message will be something you state in your presentation and may even repeat throughout your presentation; in other cases the message will be implied, based upon the key points being shared.

Some presenters make the mistake of thinking that their message needs to be detailed and complex. They are afraid that if a message is too simple it might not be taken seriously. A few years ago I was delivering 'elevator pitch' training in the Tyndall Research Institute in Cork.[1] I asked a group of attendees to describe Tyndall in no more than fifty words. It took a few minutes to complete and they were pleased with their efforts. I then asked them to cut it down to twenty-five words. It got interesting as they discussed what words or phrases to remove. After a few minutes they had it cut down to twenty-five words and again were pleased with their effort. I then asked them to cut it down to six words. After they finished cursing me for asking them to do this, they set about their task. It took longer as they struggled to agree what words to remove. Eventually they settled on the following 'Tyndall: where research meets industry'. As a message that captures what Tyndall represents, it is damn near perfect. So, to conclude, the message should be short and to the point, in order to capture the essence of what you are trying to say in a way that is easy for your audience to understand.

TRUE Criteria (40 pts)

A clear message meets the four TRUE criteria. A message that is clear will contribute to the audience's thinking, will be easy

---

1 An elevator pitch is a thirty second to two minute explanation of your business. It is called an elevator pitch because it is meant to be what you would say to your ideal client if you found yourself travelling in an elevator with them. The journey is short, so the pitch is designed to deliver a message that piques their curiosity and makes them want to find out more.

to understand and recall, and will help to keep the audience engaged during the presentation.

A single message

I will often ask an audience the following question. How many messages should your presentation have if it is five minutes, fifteen minutes or fifty-five minutes long? Not surprisingly, the answers I usually receive vary depending on the length of the presentation. This is a commonly made mistake – in fact the number of messages that any presentation should have, regardless of length, is one. The longer the presentation the more points you can have to support that message, or the deeper you can go into each point, but for each presentation there should only be one message. Remember, your job as a presenter is to get your message across to your audience. It will be easier for them to remember the message if they have only one to remember.

TRUE Criteria (40 pts)

A single message meets the four TRUE criteria. A single message will be easier to recall and understand. It will give the presenter a better chance of contributing to the thinking of their audience, which will make it easier to keep them engaged.

Key points

Having decided on the message you want to deliver, you now need to select the material that will support the message. There is no set rule but somewhere between three and five key points is a reasonable guide. There should be enough of them to get your message across and ensure that it is heard and understood, and yet few enough that the audience won't switch off. Any more than this and a presentation runs the risk of becoming confusing, or too long, which could cause your audience to lose interest. Ideally, these points will be delivered on different subjects that reinforce the message you are trying to get across and will be kept separate from each other (choosing an appropriate roadmap will help). For example, if I was delivering a presentation aimed at persuading a client to choose me as their supplier of choice, the different subjects covered might include marketing support, competitive pricing and product training. This will allow the audience to distinguish one point from another.

TRUE Criteria (30 pts)

Having three to five clear points meets three of the TRUE criteria. Delivering a presentation with a number of clearly distinguishable key points makes your presentation easier to understand, engage with and recall.

An agenda (outline of presentation)

A presentation is a medium for sharing a message. Audiences should be focused on the message and not on the medium itself. For that reason I believe that including an agenda in your presentation – and by that I mean giving a verbal outline of how the presentation will proceed or what areas you are going to speak about – will make a presentation easy to follow and allow your audience to spend their time thinking about your message and not the medium in which you are sharing that message.

An agenda should set out clearly what the presenter is going to talk about. It should also give an indication of the length of time the presentation will take and state the outcomes the audience can expect from the presentation.

TRUE Criteria (20 pts)

Having a clear agenda or outline of the presentation meets two of the TRUE criteria. It contributes to the audience's thinking and makes the presentation easier to understand.

DON'TS

Too much information

Some presenters put too much information into a presentation. They believe that the more information you give your audience the easier it will be to understand the message you are trying to get across. In reality, the opposite is true.

As an expert on their subject, a presenter will always have more information available to them than they can fit into the presentation. The danger is that many presenters provide too much information, believing that this will improve their presentation. This is commonly referred to as a 'data dump' and usually bores an audience to death. When it comes to presentations, less is better.

TRUE Criteria (-40 pts)

Too much information meets none of the TRUE criteria. It won't make a presentation easier to recall or understand. It will hinder audience engagement and probably cause them to switch off and spend less time thinking about your message because they will have to work too hard to figure out what your message is.

Lack of a clear message (multiple messages)

As well as sometimes putting too much information into their presentation, presenters can also include too many messages. The thinking is that the more messages they have in their presentation, the better the chance of audience members remembering some part of it. However, this really doesn't work. Too many messages leads to confused audiences and confused audiences tend to stop listening altogether.

TRUE Criteria (-40 pts)

Having too many messages meets none of the TRUE criteria. Too many messages make a presentation more difficult to understand and recall. It also makes engaging with your audience more difficult, which, in turn, stops them from thinking about your presentation because it is too much like hard work.

PRESENTATION SCORECARD			
Body of Presentation	**Points**	**True Criteria**	**My Score**
A clear message	40	TRUE	
A single message	40	TRUE	
3 to 5 key points	30	RUE	
Agenda	20	TU	
Too much information	- 40		
Lack of a clear message (multiple messages)	- 40		

7

ENGAGING YOUR AUDIENCE

Audiences need to feel that they are part of your presentation. They need to believe that you are having a conversation with them that they can contribute to, even if they don't contribute out loud. In many ways the aim of a presenter is to get the audience to contribute to the presentation inside the confines of their own head. This means getting your audience to think about your presentation and how it can benefit them. It means delivering the presentation in a way that resonates with them and making sure that they don't get distracted and start thinking about something else.

To do this, presenters need to employ 'audience engagement techniques'. These are elements in presentations that will make some parts of your presentation stand out from the whole, which are then easier to recall a week later because of how they connected with the audience. Collectively they contribute significantly to meeting the TRUE criteria.

In a twenty-minute presentation a presenter will use between 2,500 and 3,000 words and the reality is that most of these words will be forgotten almost as soon as they have been said. The challenge is how as a presenter, when your words are being forgotten, do you make sure your message is remembered?

Audience engagement techniques work because they

generate a reaction in the audience. Whether that reaction is physical, emotional or intellectual, it is more easily remembered than words. If you ask an audience what they can remember about a presentation a week after they heard it, the first thing they will recall is something that applied directly to themselves. It might be that they laughed, or carried out a physical action, or made sense of something the presenter said that they then applied to their own personal circumstances. Once they recall their reaction, they can remember the relevance of that reaction and that helps them to remember your message.

As a presenter you can apply audience engagement techniques as follows:

1. By what you say. It might be a turn of phrase that stands out. It might be a phrase that is pleasant on the ear, making it memorable. Think of some of the stand-out phrases attributed to the likes of Mark Twain. For example, 'It is better to keep your mouth shut and appear stupid, than open it and remove all doubt.' We remember what was said because of how it was phrased.

2. By how you make your audience feel. If you say something that disgusts them, makes them angry, makes them happy or sad, or catches them by surprise, a week later they will remember that feeling more quickly than the words that generated it. Once they recall that feeling, it will be easier to recall the words, which in turn will help them remember the message.

3. By getting your audience to do something physically. A week later they will find it easier to remember something they did than something you said and, when they do, it will help them to remember why they were asked to do it, which will make it easier to recall your message.

4. By connecting your message to something they are already familiar with. Attaching your message to something that already resides within their existing bank of knowledge allows them to make sense of your message and makes it easier to recall. A week later if they are trying to recall your message, they will recall what they are already familiar with first and that will help them remember your message. The 'Law of Contiguity' states that 'when two ideas or psychologically perceived events have once occurred in close association, they are likely to occur in close association again, the subsequent occurrence of one tending to elicit the other'.[1] Attaching your message to something your audience is already familiar with will keep them linked going forward and each time they recall one they will recall the other.

In my experience, most sales professionals don't take the time to coat their presentation with these techniques. They focus solely on the message they want to get across without ever considering how to make sure it is listened to, understood and

---

1 Garavan, T. N., Hogan, C. and Cahir-Donnell, A., *Making Training & Development Work: A Best Practice Guide* (Oak Tree Press, 2003).

remembered. In this chapter I am going to share audience engagement techniques that will connect your audience to your presentation and make it easier for them to remember, understand and buy into it. I will also share some of the techniques that presenters use that hinder audience connection.

TECHNIQUES TO ENGAGE YOUR AUDIENCE
Humour

Humour is a powerful tool for sales professionals. Victor Borge once said, 'Laughter is the shortest distance between two people.' Making an audience laugh, in an appropriate manner, goes a long way towards helping a presenter connect with them. An audience's laughter is a signal of their acceptance of the presenter or the presenter's point of view. This acceptance makes it easier for them to buy into a presenter's ideas.

Laughter is an internal reaction to an external stimulus and when trying to recall the details of a presentation a day, a week or a month after it was delivered, we find it easier to remember our internal reactions. Once we remember the internal reaction it becomes easier to remember the information that generated that reaction.

Humour engages an audience and holds their attention. That said, for many presenters, making an audience laugh can be challenging. Some presenters believe that they are not funny, while others are afraid that audiences won't laugh where they are supposed to. The good news is that anyone can learn to be funnier, can learn how to inject humour into presentations. Of course, sometimes audiences won't laugh when you want them to and will laugh when you weren't expecting them to. That said, the reward when you get an audience to laugh is definitely worth the risk. I will share a number of techniques in Chapter 8 that a presenter can use to help inject humour into a presentation.

TRUE Criteria (30 pts)

Humour meets three of the TRUE criteria. It aids recall, understanding and engages audiences.

A story

Stories are the most powerful tool a presenter can use when creating a presentation to meet the TRUE criteria. Nothing connects as effectively, aids recall, promotes understanding or captures an audience's attention with the same impact as a well-told story.

Stories are part of our DNA. It is how we have transferred information and learning for thousands of years. It is one of the first mediums we use to teach children from an early age and it is the medium we use to share information on a daily basis and yet, for some reason, when it comes to delivering presentations, we choose not to apply this tried and tested method. Instead we stick to facts, figures and statistics (more about these below). Stories connect emotionally and are more powerful for doing so. They are so powerful that they merit their own chapter (see Chapter 9).

TRUE Criteria (40 pts)

Stories meet the four TRUE criteria. They contribute to the

audience's thinking, aid recall and understanding, and engage audiences.

Dialogue

Dialogue is a tool that can be used by a presenter to reinforce a point they are trying to make. It works when the presenter decides to become the person or persons in the example they are using to make that point. Instead of just giving the example as something that happened in the past, dialogue allows the presenter to deliver the example as if it is taking place in front of the audience. This changes how the audience receives it. They become more active when they feel that the story is unfolding in front of them and this increases the impact of the message.

As an example of dialogue, I tell a story about my eight-year-old nephew. I use this story to illustrate that on occasion we can all make an assumption that we know the correct answer to a question or problem, but then discover that our assumption is wrong. The story goes like this: One day my nephew was sitting at the dinner table with the rest of his family when his mother decided to explain who the Suffragettes were. She looked at him and said, 'There was a time in history when men could vote and women couldn't and a group of women got together to address this terrible injustice.' She then asked her son a question: 'Do you know what those women were called?' Her son looked at her confidently and said, 'I do, mum. They were called prostitutes.'

When giving this example I become the mother (and give her a distinctive voice) and deliver her words as if I am her. I then become the son (and give him a different voice) and deliver his reply as if I am him. The dialogue brings the example to life in front of the audience, which increases the impact of the message.

TRUE Criteria (20 pts)

Using dialogue in a presentation meets two of the TRUE criteria. It engages audiences and aids recall.

A question

Questions are a powerful tool for engaging your audience. Questions get them thinking, and when they are doing that they are fully focused on your topic. Presenters can ask questions that require the audience to answer verbally, to answer with a gesture or action, or just to consider the answer in their own heads. Questions promote understanding, as they allow the audience to derive their own answers. They also make your message easier to remember because it makes them active participants in your presentation.

A full range of questions are available to the presenter, from closed questions that generate a 'yes' or 'no' answer, to open questions that require a more detailed answer.[2] Probing

---

2 Closed questions are questions that start with words such as 'could', 'should', 'would', 'have', 'does', 'can' and 'are'. One of my favourite closed questions when delivering a presentation is 'Does that make sense?' I will ask it after I have made a particular point and want to make sure I have explained it clearly enough for my audience.

Open questions begin with words such as 'what', 'why', 'how', 'which', 'where', 'who' and 'when'. An example of an open question that I ask my attendees at the beginning of a training day is 'What would you like to take away from today?' Each attendee provides a fairly detailed answer to this question, which gives me information that I can use to tailor the training to meet their needs.

questions such as 'What exactly do you mean by …?' can also be asked, or hypothetical questions such as 'What would happen if …?' or 'How would we handle the following situation?'

TRUE Criteria (20 pts)

Questions meet two of the TRUE criteria. They cause audiences to think, both about the question and its answer, and because of this they engage with the presentation. When asked a question we focus on that question.

Audience involvement

Getting your audience to physically do something during your presentation is a very effective means of engaging them. It also helps to create understanding and makes your message easier to remember.

There are many techniques for getting your audience to do something during a presentation. For example when demonstrating how easy it is for our message to be misunderstood, I will often ask audiences to tear a piece of paper by following a set of instructions. I give everyone a plain sheet of A4 paper and ask them to hold the sheet in both hands and close their eyes. I then ask them to fold the piece of paper in half and, once done, ask them to tear off the right-hand corner. They repeat the action of folding and tearing another three times. They then open out their sheet of paper, open their eyes and hold up the sheet for everyone to see. In spite of the fact that everyone received the same instructions the audience members always end up with a plethora of vastly different results. There are two reasons for this. The first reason is due to how they interpret my instructions and the second is due to the lack of clarity of those instructions.

Another useful audience participation exercise is to ask members of the audience to draw an image on a flip chart. (See the next section, 'Concrete Images', for examples of the types of images I ask audience members to draw and how these can be applied to the message.)

There are many different types of activities available to a presenter. Spending a little bit of time finding appropriate activities and practising getting comfortable with using them will add significantly to the impact of your presentation. I have had audience members meet me months later and comment that they can still remember the activity or action I asked them to get involved in.

TRUE Criteria (30 pts)

Getting your audience to physically do something meets three of the TRUE criteria. It aids recall, it helps to promote understanding and it engages.

Concrete images

In their book, *Made to Stick*, Dan and Chip Heath talk about the benefit of using concrete images as a tool for bringing clarity to a message.[3]

---

3 Heath, C. and Heath, D., *Made to Stick: Why Some Ideas Survive and Others Die* (Random House, New York, 2007).

When I am delivering a TRUE Presentation Skills training programme I will at some stage call four attendees up to the top of the room. I will give them an index card with one word on it and ask them to draw a picture of that word on the flip chart. Typically two of the words I put onto an index card are the words 'bicycle' and 'sunflower'. The attendee then draws an image of the word they have been given and the audience are asked to shout out the answer as soon as they recognise what the attendee is drawing. Audiences always recognise the bicycle long before the person has finished drawing it. They always recognise the sunflower, although it takes a little longer to get than the bicycle.

On the other index cards I will write down words that are relevant to the organisation or the attendees themselves. I will select words like 'strategy', 'process' and 'investment' and ask an attendee to draw these types of words. More often than not the audience struggle and fail to recognise what is being drawn. It is also very noticeable that the person doing the drawing usually struggles to work out how to visually depict these types of words. Think about it – how would you draw 'strategy'? Nothing comes readily to mind, does it? And if it doesn't come easily to you as the presenter, it is going to be difficult to articulate the idea behind the word to your audience with real clarity.

Using concrete images can help to bring clarity to the message a presenter is making a) because they are a physical image that people are already familiar with, and b) since we are already familiar with the image, we are drawing on an existing bank of knowledge to help make sense of what the presenter is saying. We are drawing on recall. We search an internal file to help us identify the image.

Concrete images are an effective element because they allow a presenter to take the information they want to share (information which is often unfamiliar to their audience) and marry it to something that they are familiar with. It is this marriage that allows the audience to make sense of the point the presenter is looking to get across, because they can see the point in a form they already understand.

Let me give you an example. A couple of years ago, I was working with an insurance company on one of their presentations. My task was to analyse their existing presentation and identify ways in which their message could be made more engaging and persuasive. One section of this presentation was focused on 'Investments' and within this section they wanted to talk about how they could carry out a risk profile of potential investors that would allow them to match the right type of investment to the level of risk an investor would be comfortable with.

There were seven different levels of risk and one of the presenters insisted on going into the fine detail of each type of investment for each of the levels of risk. He spoke in detail about investments that were at one end of the scale, low risk and low yield, right through to the other end of the scale where the investments were potentially very high yield and very high risk. As content it was dull, dry and boring. It contained abstract and unfamiliar ideas, as well as industry jargon. In short it made very little sense to the audience and did nothing to keep them engaged.

Thankfully the presenter was open to making changes. I asked him to change the presentation by making reference to the seven levels of risk but not going into them in detail. We then added the following. I asked him to equate each level of investment risk to an equivalent level of physical risk. Here's what we came up with. For the investment with the lowest level of risk and yield I asked the presenter to compare it to two people sitting on a park bench in Central Park playing a game of chess. This is an activity that most people are familiar with and would recognise as being of low physical risk. At the other end of the scale I asked the presenter to compare the very high-risk investments to Felix Baumgartner, the Austrian who jumped from the edge of space in October 2012. The images allowed the audience to identify easily the level of financial risk they would be comfortable taking, by equating it with a recognisable level, from low to high, of physical risk.

TRUE Criteria (40 pts)

Concrete images meet the four TRUE criteria. They contribute to the audience's thinking, aid recall and help to promote understanding and engage audiences.

Simile

This is a rhetorical device in which something is described as being 'like' or 'as' something else. Presenters use it by taking something unknown (their content and message) and marrying it to something the audience is already familiar with. This marriage helps the audience make sense of the point being made. Often something from nature can be very effective. For example, a presenter might describe an organisation as being like a large tree. The organisation's headquarters is like the trunk of the tree and their offices are each like one of the tree's branches. The familiarity that most of us have with large trees with an array of branches helps us to make sense of the structure of this organisation. The key to an effective simile is to keep the 'something else' as simple as possible. Simile is something we use every day to clarify our message. We describe people as being as 'bold as brass', as 'quiet as a mouse', as 'blind as a bat'. Good presenters do the same.

TRUE Criteria (40 pts)

Similes meet the four TRUE criteria. They contribute to the audience's thinking, aid recall and help to promote understanding and engage audiences.

Contrast

Contrast is a technique in which the second part of a sentence sounds like the reverse of the first part of the sentence. It makes a sentence stand out, thereby making it easier to remember, and it also helps to make the presenter's message easier to remember. The most memorable example of this is probably the line from John F. Kennedy's inaugural address as president of the United States of America in 1961: 'And so my fellow Americans, ask not what your country can do for you – ask what you can do for your country.' Kennedy's line is one of the most memorable and often quoted examples of the contrast technique.

Here is an example of how I have used contrast. When I am delivering training on TRUE presentations, I constantly stress the importance of using stories to get a message across. I encourage attendees to collect and stockpile stories they hear that resonate with them. We never know when a story we have heard in the past will be suitable for getting a point across in the future, so it is best to collect them when you hear them, even if you never get to use them. Sometimes I get asked, 'What is the point of collecting stories if they are not going to be used?' My answer is, 'It is better to have them and not need them, than to need them and not have them.'

TRUE Criteria (20 pts)

Contrast meets two of the TRUE criteria. It engages the audience and aids recall.

Echo

As the name suggests, this technique involves repeating a word or phrase a number of times throughout your presentation. This word or phrase should be your key message delivered in one sentence. The purpose is to reinforce this key phrase/message in the mind of the audience. A day, a week, a month after the presentation this one phrase might be the only thing your audience can remember because they heard it repeated a number of times.

A number of years ago I delivered a short seven-minute speech that was entitled 'Life's too short'. During the seven minutes I used the phrase 'Life's too short' seven times. This was my key message and my aim was to ensure that my audience would remember this phrase even if they remembered nothing else.

TRUE Criteria (20 pts)

Echo meets two of the TRUE criteria. It aids recall and understanding.

Alliteration

This is a great technique for making a sentence stand out and easier to remember. It involves starting every word of a sentence (or nearly every word of a sentence) with the same letter. An old children's nursery rhyme goes like this: 'Betty bought a bit of butter, but the bit of butter Betty bought was bitter so Betty bought a better bit of butter to make the bit of bitter butter better'. I learned that as a six year old and can remember it clearly all these years later. Tabloid newspapers often use alliteration in their front-page headlines. They are looking for something short and snappy that will catch the attention of a person who glances at it and make it easier to remember and, in their case, prompt the passer-by to purchase a copy of the paper. In presentations it can be particularly useful when used in the title, for example: 'Six strategies for sales success', or 'How to prepare and present powerful persuasive presentations'.

TRUE Criteria (20 pts)

Alliteration meets two of the TRUE criteria. It engages audiences and aids recall.

Metaphor

A metaphor is when we describe something or someone as being something else. This differs from a simile in that instead of describing something as being 'like' or 'as' something else, a metaphor transfers the sense or aspects of one thing to another. For example, once in a speech I described a sunflower as being very tall, thin and fragile. I asked the audience to imagine how easily the sunflower would bend and break if a strong wind came howling through the garden in which it was growing. I then said that my friend Joan 'was our sunflower'. This allowed my audience to create a clear picture of the physical appearance and fragility of my friend in their heads.

Metaphors such as this allow our audience to make sense of what we are speaking about because we have married it to something with which they are already familiar.

TRUE Criteria (40 pts)

Metaphors meet the four TRUE criteria. They contribute to the audience's thinking, aid recall and help to promote understanding and engage audiences.

Appealing to the senses

We all process information through our different senses (what we see, hear, smell, do) and we all have preferences about how we receive information. Some people find it easier to process information when they have received it visually, others find it easier to process information when they have to physically do something to receive it and some people find it easier to process information that they hear. The key from a presenter's perspective is to recognise that in any audience there will be people who prefer to receive information in each of these different ways and it is important that we make sure our message is delivered to reflect these preferences. These preferences are outlined below.

Visual engagement

Used correctly, the likes of PowerPoint, Prezi and Keynote are wonderful tools and great assets to a presenter (the important words in this sentence are 'used correctly'). These tools can offer a visual support to the words being expressed. They bring clarity and understanding to those words and the combination of words and visual imagery reinforces the presenter's message, engages the audience more effectively and makes it easier for the audience to remember the points being made.

An audience's understanding and recall increases significantly when presenters deliver their message towards both the ear and the eye of those listening, rather than presenting it only for the ear.

TRUE Criteria (20 pts)

Used correctly visual engagement meets two of the TRUE criteria. It helps to engage the audience and create understanding.

Auditory engagement

It might seem strange referencing what an audience hears as an engagement technique when presentations are typically delivered orally, but as presenters the words we use have the power to bore our audiences to death or inspire them to take action. Auditory engagement is about inspiring action. It is about using our words to connect emotionally, to create pictures in the mind of the listener and to construct sentences in such a way that their flow appeals to the ear of the listener. Of the three senses referred to in this section, my personal preference is auditory engagement. I love listening to a presenter who has taken the time to construct their words and language for the purpose of engaging their audience. I love listening to a presenter and suddenly realising that, in my own mind, I have constructed a picture based on the words I have heard, and I love hearing a well-crafted phrase and realising how that phrase has connected with me because of its construction. The following is a quote from Rosa Parks. It is in two sentences and you will see (and hear) how each are constructed to appeal to the ear of the listener: 'Stand for something or you will fall for anything. Today's mighty oak is yesterday's nut that held its ground.'

TRUE Criteria (20 pts)

In the context of how people process information, auditory engagement meets two of the TRUE criteria. It helps to engage the audience and create understanding.

Kinaesthetic engagement

Kinaesthetic engagement involves getting your audience to learn through physical activities rather than by listening passively to a presenter. Getting your audience to physically do something has the potential to reinforce the message you are trying to get across and promote understanding of the idea, product or service you are speaking about.

Sales professionals use this technique all the time. They will visit clients with samples that the client will be encouraged to hold and play with to get a better understanding of how the product works. For example, take a sales professional who sells head shields for welding that darken automatically once a welder has struck an arc to begin welding. Putting that into the hands of a welder, allowing them to try it out, will allow them to get an understanding of how the head shield performs. They will be able to turn knobs on the shield to see the different levels of eye protection available. It will allow them to understand how to switch the shield's setting from a welding application to a grinding application. It will allow them to understand the adjustment of the head cradle so that they can make it as comfortable for themselves as possible.

Coming up with an appropriate physical activity for your client or audience to do during your presentation, like the tearing the paper exercise I mentioned earlier, or drawing the bicycle on the flip chart, will make it much easier for them to recall that action a day, week or month later, and this, in turn, will help them to recall your message.

TRUE Criteria (30 pts)

Used correctly, kinaesthetic engagement meets three of the TRUE criteria. It helps to engage the audience, creates understanding and aids recall.

Props

The real benefit of using a prop in a presentation is twofold. Firstly, it reinforces a message, bringing clarity to the point you are aiming to get across. Secondly, it mixes up the way in which the message is being delivered. If your audience has been listening to you for a period of time, showing them a prop reinvigorates their thinking because they are now being exposed to a visual stimulus instead of, or as well as, an auditory one.

A few years ago, in my 'Life's too short' presentation that I mentioned earlier, I used an Easter egg as a prop. When the speech was finished a lady walked up to me and said, 'Eric, great speech. Now do me a favour, open the egg.' I have met that person a number of times since, and each time I do, the first thing she asks is if I have any chocolate with me. It has become a running joke. Now you might ask how this helps her remember my message from a few years ago, and the honest answer is I don't know if it does because I haven't asked her. But here's what I do know: the Easter egg generated an internal reaction within that person that day and it is that internal reaction that gives me the best opportunity of having my message remembered.

TRUE Criteria (30 pts)

Using relevant props meets three of the TRUE criteria. It helps to engage the audience, creates understanding and aids recall.

Choosing the most relevant content

Choosing the most relevant content is crucial to creating a great presentation. Having completed the brainstorming session in the pre-presentation phase you now have far more information than you need or could possibly use. Choosing the most relevant content means working through the ideas you have gathered to identify which ones will best support the message you are looking to get across. This means looking at these ideas with a cold clinical eye and being prepared to discard most of them. There have been occasions when preparing presentations that I have brainstormed more than 100 ideas that could potentially have been used in a presentation, but ended up selecting only the most relevant twenty. The twenty ideas included not only the content but also the methods by which the information would be delivered in the presentation. That included choosing the audience engagement elements to get the message across. Everything else was discarded.

TRUE Criteria (40 pts)

Content edited prior to delivery of the presentation meets the four TRUE criteria. It means that you have included only the most suitable material for that audience, which will aid engagement, understanding and recall. It should also make it easier to keep your audience focused on your message and keep them thinking about how you can help them.

Rhetorical devices (acronyms, anaphora)

Rhetorical devices are language techniques used to achieve a particular emphasis and effect, and are a great way to deliver content in your presentation so that it stands out and is easier to remember. Using a rhetorical device in a presentation is like taking a single word in a written sentence, highlighting the word in **bold** and changing the colour of the word.

Long after the presentation has been heard the rhetorical device might be one of the few elements that your audience can recall because of how it sounded, flowed or stood out from everything else.

There are many examples of rhetorical devices.[4] One such example is an acronym – a word formed from the initial letters or groups of letters of the words in a set phrase or a series of words, and pronounced as a separate word. For example, the TRUE of TRUE presentations is an acronym, spelling a word made up from the first letter of the group of words that form the four criteria of great presentations. A common one used in business that you might be aware of is the term SMART, meaning specific, measurable, attainable, relevant and timely, particularly when applied to goals that the company or individual wishes to achieve.

Another example of a rhetorical device is anaphora. This is the repetition of a certain word or phrase at the beginning of successive lines of your presentation. Martin Luther King used this technique powerfully throughout his 'I have a dream' speech. At one point he starts eight sentences in a row with the phrase 'I have a dream'. In another section, he starts three sentences with the words, 'With this faith'. Near the end of the speech he uses the phrase, 'Let freedom ring' to great effect. He says, 'Let freedom ring from the mighty mountains of New York. Let free-

---

4 Simile, contrast, echo, alliteration and metaphor, which are mentioned earlier in this chapter, are all examples of rhetorical devices.

dom ring from the heightening Alleghenies of Pennsylvania! Let freedom ring from the snowcapped Rockies of Colorado!' In total he uses this phrase ten times. The anaphora does not mean an audience will remember your entire presentation, but it can help them remember the overriding message.

Rhetorical devices make sentences and phrases stand out so they are easier to remember after they are delivered. They help engage audiences because a phrase that stands out has a greater chance of resonating with them. Sometimes, when we hear a phrase that stands out, we take the time to just enjoy the flow of the words. When we do that we are not distracted by anything else.

TRUE Criteria (10 pts)
Rhetorical devices meet one of the TRUE criteria in that they aid recall. They make it easier for the audience to remember something you said during the presentation, which can help them to remember your message.

'Them' focused
Some presenters refer to this engagement technique as being 'you' focused. I refer to it as being 'them' focused. 'Them' is the audience. Your presentation is all about them, all for them.

Many presenters, particularly those who are nervous, tend to focus on themselves. They worry about how they will perform. They worry about making mistakes, letting themselves or others down. Presenters who are focused on themselves tend to deliver their presentation from their own perspective. They use language and sentences that are driven from their own perspective. They see things only from their own point of view. What these presenters are doing is the equivalent of focusing on the features of a product when the audience wants to know about its benefits.

Your audience doesn't care about you or your message. What they care about is how you or your message can help them. As a presenter it is imperative that you deliver a presentation in terms of how you can help your audience. By doing so you have a greater chance of engaging them and getting them thinking about how they can use your product, service or message.

The right audience will be more interested in a phrase like 'I can help you grow your sales by 30 per cent' than by 'I deliver sales training courses', although the latter phrase is often how presenters structure their content. The challenge for presenters is to know how to change the language they use from focusing on themselves to focusing on their audience. One simple way is not to use words like 'I', 'my' and 'ours', when sentences that include words like 'you' and 'yours' would resonate more effectively.

TRUE Criteria (40 pts)

Being focused on 'them' meets the four TRUE criteria. Presenters who focus on 'them', the audience, and deliver the message in language that is designed for that audience and not focused on themselves, will be more engaging, will deliver a message that is easier to understand and recall, and will craft a presentation that gets your audience thinking about how you can help them.

Emotional connection

If you want to connect with your audience and want to get them to buy into your ideas, you have to connect with them on an emotional level. Logic alone is not enough. This can be difficult in a business environment. Business is built around facts, figures, statistics and data. We need to be able to measure progress and change and, because of this, presenters tend to deliver presentations that are heavy on these facts and figures, etc. The result of presentations built solely on facts and data is an audience that gets bored very easily and switches off. If logic alone worked, then every time a utilities sales person called to your door offering you cheaper gas or electricity you would immediately sign up. In reality, only one in ten signs up.

Connecting emotionally means making your audience 'feel' something about you or your message. It means getting them to like you or like your idea. It means getting them to feel they would be better off with your product or service. The emotion we all feel is an internal guide that acts as an internal influencer. Connecting emotionally allows a presenter to influence that internal guide.

So how can a presenter connect emotionally with an audience? 1) Include stories in your presentation that support or illustrate the facts and figures. 2) Focus on the audience and use language that resonates with them. Deliver your message from their perspective. Talk about how they can benefit from what you do, not about what you do. If you are delivering a presentation about a product or service, talk about the benefits and results, not about the features or actions. When you talk about how an audience can benefit from using a product or service, members of the audience have their own internal conversation in which they will make sense of your offering and justify any action they take. Even if you are speaking to an audience you have never met before, it is possible to find out information about them that can be applied to tailor the content of the presentation.[5] 3) Make eye contact with members of your audience. It is a strong emotional connector.

TRUE Criteria (40 pts)

Connecting emotionally meets the four TRUE criteria. It engages the audience, gets them thinking about your product or service and how it can benefit them. It makes your message easier to understand and remember. While audiences might not remember exactly what you said, they will remember how they felt during your presentation. That feeling is an internal reaction and when they recall it, it will help them to remember the words or message that generated it.

WHAT NOT TO DO

No stories

A story is the single most effective way to connect with your audience yet in business and sales presentations most presenters stay away from them. They believe that they should stick solely

---

5 For example, if you are speaking to an association or at a conference, it should be possible to get the names of some of attendees in advance and call them to get an understanding of what is important to them. When I am speaking at events or delivering training, I will, where possible, get permission to contact some of the attendees in advance to find out what content they would like me to cover.

to the facts, figures and statistics. By doing so they miss an opportunity to connect on an emotional level with the audience, and, as we have just seen, most people make decisions based upon emotion, not facts, figures and statistics. Presentations that are devoid of stories are also dull and can cause audiences to switch off, which makes getting the message across to them more difficult. It also makes it harder for them to recall the message at a later time.

TRUE Criteria (-40 pts)

Having no stories in a presentation will reduce engagement, understanding and recall.

Abstract ideas

An abstract idea is one that is hard to describe. It is something that is difficult to explain in a way that makes sense to the people listening. Abstract ideas are the type of ideas that you would find difficult to draw on a flip chart (the opposite of concrete images). Attendees on the TRUE presentations training course find it very difficult to draw a visual representation of words such as 'strategy', 'investment' or 'risk' and their audience finds it nearly impossible to identify what they are drawing. We inevitably get a varied range of guesses as to what the picture embodies. Eventually, I will stop the exercise, tell the audience what the words were and ask them to consider how difficult it must be for your audience to make sense of your intended point if you are struggling to explain it in terms anyone can understand. If you are talking about an abstract idea, ask yourself if it could be explained better with a concrete image or with the use of a simile or metaphor.

TRUE Criteria (-40 pts)

Abstract ideas are difficult to follow. They stop audiences from thinking about your message, hinder understanding and engagement, thereby causing audiences to switch off and stop listening. A day, a week, a month later they cannot recall your message because they didn't actually hear it when the presentation was being delivered.

Overreliance on facts, figures and statistics

Delivering a presentation that relies solely on facts, figures and statistics will hinder a presenter's efforts to get their message across. Facts, figures and statistics are necessary for most sales presentations, but on their own they will cause your audience to become bored and switch off. We are not wired to process information this way. We struggle to make sense of them sometimes and often they cause an audience to work too hard. They provide a strictly logical argument, but human beings need the emotional connection as well.

Most business presentations rely solely on these and most audiences switch off early in the presentation and start thinking about anything other than the presenter's message. You can avoid this pitfall by making sure that you use some of the positive techniques I have outlined earlier in this chapter.

TRUE Criteria (-40 pts)

Facts, figures and statistics on their own hinder engagement, reduce understanding and recall, and stop the audience from thinking about your message.

Overly-long presentations

The longer the presentation the more difficult it is to keep your audience engaged. Presentations that are too long undoubtedly cause audiences to switch off. Some presenters think that the way to get their message across is to give their audience as much information as possible. In most cases, the reverse is true. A short and concise presentation with a clear message will outperform a longer presentation every time.

How long is too long? This is a good question. This quote by Winston Churchill should act as a guide: 'A good speech should be like a woman's skirt. Long enough to cover the subject and short enough to create interest.' A presentation that is built around a clear objective, tailored for a specific audience and crafted with a single clear message won't ever be too long.

TRUE Criteria (-40 pts)

Presentations that are too long cause audiences to stop thinking about your message, make your message more difficult to understand and remember, and cause audiences to disengage completely.

PRESENTATION SCORECARD			
Audience Engagement	**Points**	**TRUE Criteria**	**My Score**
Humour	30	RUE	
A story	40	TRUE	
Dialogue	20	RE	
A question	20	TE	
Audience involvement	30	RUE	
Concrete images	40	TRUE	
Simile	40	TRUE	
Contrast	20	RE	
Echo	20	RU	
Alliteration	20	RE	
Metaphor	40	TRUE	
Visual engagement	20	UE	
Auditory engagement	20	UE	
Kinesthetic engagement	30	RUE	
Props	30	RUE	
Choosing the most relevant content	40	TRUE	
Rhetorical devices	10	R	
'THEM' Focused	40	TRUE	
Emotional connection	40	TRUE	
No stories	- 40		
Abstract ideas	- 40		
Overreliance on facts, figures and statistics	- 40		
Overly-long presentations	- 40		

8

USING HUMOUR

Humour is one of the most underused elements in business presentations. An audience buys into the presenter as much as their message. If we don't like the presenter it will be difficult to invest in their message. Getting your audience to laugh is a powerful way to get them to like you.

The following is a list of techniques for adding humour to a presentation. These are techniques that most people use on a daily basis without ever taking the time to see them as specific techniques that can be applied deliberately to a presentation.

There are two caveats before I continue. Firstly, humour is not appropriate for every speech or presentation. If you were speaking/presenting to a group of employees about job cuts, redundancies or downsizing, humour would not be appropriate. Secondly, everybody's sense of humour is different. A good rule of thumb regarding humorous content is that if you think it might offend one person in the room it is probably best not to use the joke. You may ask, 'How can I tell if the material will offend?' There are two answers to that:

1. Rely on your gut instinct. Sometimes presenters create material that doesn't quite feel right. Their gut tells them that it might cause offence. If this occurs, don't use it. Let me give you an example. Many years ago, I delivered

a presentation to an audience made up of people from Britain, Ireland and the USA. I decided that I needed to explain to the USA attendees what currency the sales figures would be delivered in and wanted to do so in a humorous way. At the time Ireland used the Punt, so I said the following: 'The figures you are going to see are in Punts. In Ireland our currency is the Punt and we use this currency because it rhymes with ... bank manager.' I had known in advance that this was a risk and in the end it backfired horribly.

2. If you have used it before and someone has been offended, don't assume that person was wrong – don't use it again. In one particular presentation I used to tell a story about Bill Clinton, until one occasion when a lady walked up to me and informed me that she had been offended by my story. I apologised and removed the story from that presentation. Why? That lady could be the very person who might buy my product or service or recommend me to another prospective client.[1]

---

1   Here is the Clinton story (feel free to make up your own mind about its suitability). I would use this story to make the point that opportunities like this rarely come along, but when they do, you have to make the most of them: A number of years ago Bill Clinton was in Dublin to fundraise for one of Hillary's campaigns. On the Saturday morning after the fundraiser he went to Portmarnock in County Dublin to play a round of golf. My friend Gerry was in Portmarnock playing golf the same day. When Gerry stood on the first tee, Bill was on the fourth, which meant that when Gerry completed his round Clinton was already finished and back in the changing rooms. As Gerry walked into the changing rooms Bill walked out of the showers to go and get dressed. Gerry relays the story as follows. He says, 'When I saw Clinton walking out of the showers my first thought was to have a look to see what Monica found so interesting.' Gerry ended up having a ten-minute one-on-one conversation with Clinton (he didn't mention Monica).

You won't always get it right as it's not always possible to know what will offend every person in the room, but always learn from your mistakes. And if you are thinking of using humour in a presentation and want to know how effective it will be, deliver it in advance to a trusted friend who will (hopefully!) give you an honest opinion as to whether it would be funny or inappropriate.

What follows are a selection of techniques that can be used to add humour without offending and without relying on jokes.

THE CALL BACK

The call back is a reference to something that has happened or been said in the past and with which the audience is familiar. The familiarity could relate to something the audience experienced earlier in the day – or even earlier in the presentation – but can also relate to something that was said in the past about the subject matter under discussion. If delivering your presentation at a conference, it could relate to something that happened at a previous conference, or could be something connected to the theme of the conference. The call back could also be used to reference the venue being used, if something of note has happened in that venue before. As long as your audience is familiar with what happened previously you have a call back opportunity.

In February 2016 an incident occurred at the Regency Hotel in Dublin in which a man was shot and killed. It made headline news across the country and was mentioned by mainstream media in the UK. A couple of months later I had to speak at an event promoting a conference that would take place in the Regency later that year. I knew most of my audience would be familiar with the shooting and sure enough when I mentioned where the conference was going to be held it generated a less than enthusiastic response. I believed that humour was required to allay any fears that potential conference attendees might have, so I said to my audience, 'I know that some of you might be a little bit wary about attending a conference at this venue after what happened in February, but I can assure you it will be perfectly safe. I would also like to assure you that we, as the organising committee, are sensitive to your concerns. That is one of the reasons we chose not to use "bullet" points on our slides.' This line generated a little bit of laughter and helped to relax my audience.

Sometimes an attendee will arrive late for a training day I am delivering and I will often use this as a call back throughout the day. I once had someone arrive twenty minutes late for the start of a training day. They apologised profusely and I told them it was nothing to be concerned about. I took about fifteen minutes to size up my audience until I felt the call back would be well received. I used it as follows. I wanted the attendees to perform an individual exercise and the challenge was to decide who should go first, so I said: 'I need someone to go first but don't know how to decide. If only one of you had arrived late for the training.' At that point the attendees laughed because they knew who I was about to select. In this case the purpose was threefold: firstly, to generate a little bit of laughter and put the attendees as ease; secondly, to allow me to select an attendee to start the individual exercise; thirdly, to remind the attendees gently that they need to be on time (there were three further opportunities for them to be late during this training day).

SELF-DEPRECATION

When a presenter is prepared to generate a laugh at their own expense, it gives them a great chance of winning their audience's hearts and minds. When a presenter takes the 'stage' they are automatically placed in the position of being different from their audience. There are seen as an expert, invited to share their knowledge. They can be placed on a pedestal by their audience or by the person introducing them, and that is a dangerous place to be. Being seen or perceived as better as or higher up than your audience can create a barrier between presenter and audience.

Self-deprecating humour removes that barrier. Having a laugh at your own expense tells an audience that you don't take yourself too seriously and that relaxes an audience. It sends a message to your audience that you are saying that you are not any better than them and they will respond to that. (If you are ever in doubt about this, try giving a presentation from a position of arrogance where your tone and attitude suggest that you are brilliant and your audience should be grateful for the opportunity to hear you speak. Just to warn you, the reaction won't be good!)

Audiences are buying into the presenter as much as their

message. It is very difficult to buy into a message that is being delivered by someone you dislike. I'm bald and sometimes begin presentations as follows: 'Ladies and gentlemen, can everyone hear me clearly?' (This is a genuine request to ensure the audience can hear me at the back.) I then say, 'Can everyone see me? The shine off the top of my head isn't too distracting?' The audience laugh and think, 'This guy isn't taking himself too seriously.' At that point they are prepared to listen to what I have to say.

Every presenter can use self-deprecation humour. Make a list of your personal traits and characteristics. You will find plenty of opportunities to generate laughter at your own expense. Personally, I am bald, wear glasses, am the wrong side of fifty, Irish, support Tottenham Hotspur and the New York Yankees, have two children and have been married to my beautiful wife, Catherine, for more than twenty-five years. I have been mistaken for the actor Ross Kemp and been told by my youngest niece that I look like, wait for it, Gollum from *The Lord of the Rings*. There is plenty of self-deprecating material in this list. On telling people that I support Tottenham Hotspur, I will state that this obviously means I know nothing about soccer. On telling audiences that I support the New York Yankees and understand, in general terms, how the game works (which is atypical for a European), I will say something like, 'I know, some of you hadn't marked me down as being that smart.'

THE RULE OF THREE

The rule of three is a technique used by comedians. It works by playing a trick on the minds of the audience. It is a very simple and effective way for presenters to generate laughter. When applying the rule of three, a presenter makes three statements or gives three examples. The first two are similar, but the third example is completely different and unexpected.

Here's an example. The following are the three sure-fire requirements for presenters to build rapport with their audiences: 1) they must have sincerity, 2) they must have relevance, and 3) they must have brown envelopes stuffed with cash.

Here's how I believe it works. When a presenter makes their first statement or gives their first example the audience starts thinking, 'Where are they going with this?' The second statement or example answers this question. Because the audience now knows the direction in which the presenter is going, they no longer need to wait for the presenter and move ahead of them. When the third statement or example is given, however, it momentarily stops the audience in their tracks because it has taken a different direction to the one expected. This is what generates the laughter.

THE ASIDE

The aside is the telling of a funny story or incident that is only slightly connected to the presentation. The presentation does not need this story for the purpose of getting the message across; instead its purpose is to generate laughter. It is important, however, that the story is connected to the presentation in some way. It might be connected only to a single point the presenter is making, but that is enough to justify its inclusion.

It is usually prefaced with a phrase like, 'Just before I continue, I have to tell you this,' or 'Let me tell you this very quickly.' The reason it works is because the audience believe that this story has spontaneously come to the presenter and therefore it is just for them. They believe that if the presenter was giving the same presentation the next night, he or she would not include the aside. A few years ago I mentioned in a speech that I had played soccer for the Republic of Ireland and that after one particular match against Scotland I was approached by a scout from a team called Sheffield United asking me to give him a call the following week. I didn't make that call because I believed that I wasn't good enough to play professional football in England. The message of my speech was how we doubt ourselves and sometimes talk ourselves out of taking chances or trying something new. I used an aside in this speech as follows. Having relayed the part about not calling the scout because I had convinced myself I wasn't good enough, I then said, 'Before I continue, I have to tell you. I told that story to my nephew recently and he said to me, "Uncle Eric, I knew you were a good footballer and I know that's a true story", and I said to him, "How do you know it's a true story? I could be lying", and he said, "Ah no, if you were lying, you wouldn't have said it was Sheffield United."' As an aside it generated laughter (and continues to do so whenever I use it). It was connected to my speech through the football story but its sole purpose was to generate the laughter.

SIMILE

A simile is where a presenter describes something as being like something else. Usually done for the purpose of clarity, it can also be used to generate laughter. It works because that to which it is being compared is completely different or exaggerated or unconnected. To borrow an example from earlier in the book: A presentation should be like a miniskirt. Long enough to cover the essentials. Short enough to keep you interested.

MINDREADING

Mindreading is where a presenter appears to anticipate what their audience is thinking and builds that into the presentation. It generates humour because the audience appreciate that you took the time to consider how they would react or what they would be thinking, and also because they believe that this could only have been just for them. It couldn't have been for any other audience. In reality, however, it can work with any audience.

A number of years ago I delivered a presentation about creating great speeches and spoke about the commitment required. In the presentation I mentioned that I had once rewritten the same speech about twenty-three times. I told the audience that I had come up with a scale. I said that if you rewrote a speech between two and ten times, it showed that you were committed. If you rewrote your speech between eleven and fifteen times you were very committed. If you rewrote it between sixteen and twenty times you were very,

very committed and if you rewrote more than that you … At this point in my presentation someone shouted out, 'Should be committed'. Anticipating the minds of my audience, I had created a PowerPoint slide with the words 'should be committed' on it. This appeared just after the person shouted out the words. The audience roared with laughter when I put up this slide. Would I have looked foolish if they hadn't shouted out those words? Possibly, but the slide would have generated laughter on its own.

EXAGGERATION

This is a technique that can be used by presenters to magnify (or underplay) a point beyond the limits of truth. It is used for emphasis or to highlight an important or relevant point. A quick example is something like: 'If I've told you once, I've told you a million times, stop exaggerating.'

While delivering a recent training course I was explaining to the attendees how I could remember a nursery rhyme that I had learned when I was six years old and I said to them 'and I can still remember it today, twenty-five years later'. It generated laughter because there are no circumstances in which I would pass for being only thirty-one and my audience knew it. What this also demonstrates is that exaggeration works even when you don't just rely on larger numbers. Making numbers deliberately smaller will also work.

As we saw in Chapter 7, humour meets three of the TRUE criteria and is worth 30 points, by engaging audiences and aiding recall and understanding. It is a powerful tool when creating a presentation.

9

THE POWER OF STORIES

I believe that stories are the single most important element available to a presenter. They have the power to influence like no other element. So what exactly do I mean by a story? Simply put, a story is a medium for sharing a message in the very same way that an email or a company newsletter or a text message, a blog, a social media post or PowerPoint slides are mediums for message sharing. Stories just happen to do so more effectively.

Someone once said that we are all connected by the same six emotions: happiness, sadness, anger, fear, surprise and disgust. Every time a presenter tells a story that connects with one of these emotions they give themselves a great chance of connecting with their audience.

STORY FILE

Collect stories. Every day we hear stories that connect with some of the six emotions. These stories resonate with us; therefore, what presenters should be doing is collecting them. The idea is to record these stories when we don't need them, so that we have them when we do. Imagine being asked to deliver a presentation (sometimes at short notice) and having a bank of stories from which to draw and being able to select the ones that are most suitable to support your message. Would that help you to prepare better presentations faster?

Over the last few years I have collected approximately 120 stories. I have put them into a story file that I can go to every time I am creating a presentation or writing a speech. The stories are drawn from my personal and professional experiences, as well as experiences that others have shared with me.

If you want to create a story file, start by listing all of the members of your family, your friends, your work colleagues, past and present. Then list the companies you have worked for, the schools and colleges you have attended. Next list all of the places in the world you have visited and the important events in your life. Now think of a single story for each person, place or occasion that links to one of the six emotions mentioned above. We all have hundreds of stories available to us. All you need to do is write down one word, phrase or sentence that will act as a prompt for a story.

The following are phrases that I use in my story file to remind me of certain stories.

'If James Bond was a women.'

'Phillip rest in peace.'

'Ignoring Sheffield United.'

These are random phrases that help me to remember stories that might be useful for different presentations. (Are you curious?)

Let me make a suggestion. Take a few minutes right now and make a list of twenty people, places or important occasions from your life. Then think of an interesting story around each of these things. Once done, write a phrase alongside each person, place or occasion on the list. This will act as a prompt for the story.

From a sales presentation perspective these stories (and some of your personal stories may not be suitable for business presentations) will need to be married to a relevant business message. It could be a message about trust, great customer service, poor customer service, dealing with change, integrity, problem solving, etc. A number of years ago my brother Graham was working for John Player, the cigarette manufacturer, when without warning they decided to close their manufacturing facility in Dublin. Graham was devastated. At the time he was getting ready to buy an apartment and losing his job meant that couldn't happen. He spent the guts of four weeks feeling sorry for himself and then one day decided to do something he had always wanted to do. He went to Australia. Initially, he went out for a holiday but ended up living there for seven years and they were some of the happiest years of his life. I often tell this story as an example of dealing with change and seeing it as an opportunity, not a hardship. In business we often have to deal with change, whether that is market conditions, clients taking their business to a competitor, or cash-flow problems. Change is inevitable. How we deal with it is up to us.

The story file is created using an excel spreadsheet and putting a list of your business messages across the top and the story phrases down the left-hand side, then placing a mark of some kind in the corresponding box where that phrase and that business message intersect (I use a y for yes).[1] Opposite is part of my story file.

---

1 Smith P, *Lead with a Story: A Guide to Crafting Business Narratives that Captivate, Convince and Inspire* (AMACOM Books 2012) p. 272.

	Maeve putting 10 swear jar	Easter night got dumped	My birth – what my mum will tell you	Amy's birth	Louise's birth	Graham goes to Australia	Gerry meets Bill Clinton	Fiona Currachloe	Paul – hammock in Italy	1st presentation Shergar	Japanese fishermen and cormorants	Optometrist takes picture of eye	Ignoring Sheffield Utd	Playing soccer for Ireland	Dead fly	If James Bond was a woman	Sean they're called prostitutes	Phillip rest in peace
Set a vision					y											y		
Change					y	y				y								
Great customer service																		
Set goals																		
Values															y			
Collaboration											y							
Diversity																		
Set policy																		
Inspire and motivate																		
Blind courage																		
Teach important lessons									y								y	y
Provide coaching and freedom																		
Solve problems																		
Accelrate sales growth																		
Blind trust									y									
Passion for work																		
Share knowledge																		
Handle rumour and gossip																		
Encourage innovation																		
Earn respect																		
Delegate authority																		
Build a brand																		
Plan strategy																		
Who I am																		
Why I am here																		
I know what you are thinking																		
Poor customer service																		
Planning and preparation																		
Emotional connection																		
Credibility																		

I carry a pocket notebook with me all the time and whenever I hear a story that connects with me emotionally I make a note of it and stick it into my story file. There are stories in my file that I have never used but, as I previously mentioned, it is better to have them and not need them than to need them and not have them. If you make a conscious effort to collect stories, you will quickly build up a substantial story file and create a valuable resource for your presentations.

STORY COMPONENTS

Some stories will be strong enough that they can be told without referencing the message you want your audience to take away, while others would be incomplete without the message included at the end of the story. However, all business stories require a number of components to make them work for your audience. Several of these components are outlined below.

Relatable

A story must be relevant to that audience. The story must share an experience to which they can relate. Sales professionals do this very effectively when trying to persuade clients or prospects. They will often give an example of a client just like the client they are talking to, one who had a similar problem, and how they helped that client solve it. For example, a number of years ago, I worked with a sales professional who once drove 150 miles to meet a client and give him a part for a machine. It was the only way to get the part to him as the freight company that they would normally use had finished up for Christmas. I would use this story as an example of great customer service and share it with potential clients because I wanted them to know the lengths to which we would go to look after their business. I believe that a potential client would hear this story and think, 'I want to do business with a company that would do that for me.'

In saying that, a story that connects on a human level (as opposed to a business-related story) will also work. If the human story highlights a message that is relevant it can be used in a business presentation. For example, every day in business, individuals make decisions in haste and sometimes those decisions end up being wrong because they were rushed. Sales professionals will, on occasion, make promises to clients without checking that their company can deliver on that promise. They will guess at the price of a product because they want to give a prompt reply, instead of taking the time to get an accurate price, and will sometimes get the price wrong because of this.

To illustrate the danger of doing something in a rush I tell a story about Phillip. This story takes place many years ago. Phillip was in work one day when he received a phone call to say that his wife had just given birth to their first child. He panicked. He left work and ran to the shop. He bought flowers and a card. He wrote on the card. He took a bus to the hospital and when he arrived he went up two floors to the ward his wife was in. He gave her the flowers and she said, 'Thanks very much.' He gave her the card and she looked at it for a moment, then said, 'Why does the card say rest in peace?' In his haste, Phillip had bought the wrong card.

Time

Stories must be fixed in time. Children's stories tend to start with a phrase like 'A long time ago'. Business stories need to start with their equivalent of this. The business equivalent would be something like 'a couple of weeks ago' or 'on the 30 September' or 'recently' or 'in September of 2003'. An opening like this grounds the story in a specific time and place, which helps set the scene for what is to follow. It also provides context and helps an audience to make sense of what they are about to hear.

Single character

Ideally, a story will be told from the point of view of a single individual. The story will be the sharing of their experience. The benefit of telling a story about an individual is that everyone in your audience will be able to identify and connect emotionally with what the individual has experienced. Our thinking, upon hearing a story, is often either 'that could just as easily happen to me' (if something negative happened), or 'I wish that had been me' (if something good happened).

Take, for example, the story I told earlier in the book about my friend Gerry meeting Bill Clinton and having a ten-minute one-to-one conversation with the former US president. Gerry is the single character in this story. He is the person we identify with. Listening to this story unfold we can put ourselves in his shoes and imagine what having that opportunity must have been like. Most of us will be thinking, 'Fair play to him for having the confidence to engage with Bill Clinton and make the most of the opportunity.'

On the other hand, imagine if that story had unfolded differently. Imagine if Gerry hadn't been that type of person and hadn't had the confidence to engage with Clinton. Now we'd be thinking, 'What a missed opportunity.' Some of us might also be thinking, 'How would I have reacted in that scenario? Would I have had the confidence to engage with him?' Whether the story speaks of an opportunity taken or missed, we are drawn into it.

Not all stories can be built around an individual, of course. Some will be built around teams because the message is aimed at getting a team working together more effectively (sporting analogies can be useful), while others will be built around organisations. You might tell a story about an organisation and how they implemented change as a way to illustrate how you would like your organisation to change. That said, in my opinion, stories told about individuals are more powerful and effective. The key is to identify which is most relevant to the message you are looking to get across.

Three parts of an effective story

There are three parts to the most effective stories.

The first part of the story sets the scene. It provides the background or context for the rest of the story, for example, 'I was at work one day when the phone rang.' This allows your audience to make sense of what is to follow.

The second part provides the action of the story. This is the part of the story that has the potential to generate a reaction in your audience. However, don't be misled by the word 'action'.

It doesn't have to be built around a physical action. In story terms, 'action' also means the emotional experience with which your audience can identify. In the story about my eight-year-old nephew (see Chapter 7) the action occurs when he is asked a question and provides the wrong answer.

The third part provides resolution. If, for example, the second part of a story spoke of a problem that an individual experienced, such as a problem with a client, then the final part of the story explains how that problem was solved.

Sometimes a story will only have a natural first and second part. In this case the third part is the message or point the presenter wants their audience to take away. My eight-year-old nephew's story has only a first and second part: setting the scene and the action. There is no resolution. Whenever I use this story I add the third part by asking my audience if they have ever made an assumption about something only to find out that their assumption was wrong. This third part is the connecting of the story to the message I want my audience to take away from this story.

Some people believe that all stories must have conflict, that they must have a problem which the story provides a solution to. However, business stories are capable of delivering or supporting a message without having conflict in them.

Must be true

Business stories must be largely true. They must have credibility. They must be the type of story that could be checked out by your audience after you have told it and be found to be mainly true.

Telling a story does, however, allow for a little bit of poetic licence. It is not always possible to remember a story exactly as it happened and it can become embellished in places. In the main, however, it should be true. A story should be the sharing of an experience that has taken place and not something made up solely for the purpose of making an impact on your audience. In my experience, audiences are very adept at spotting stories or information that isn't true, so it is better to stick to the truth.

Must be concise

The most effective stories share an experience and deliver a message or point in the most concise manner possible. The purpose of the story is to share an experience that will connect with the audience. They only require the essentials of the story (the three parts) to do so. They do not need every tiny detail. If a story is too detailed it will lose its impact. If it is too long it will bore an audience. Business stories need to be concise and to the point.

CRAFTING AND EDITING STORIES

Everybody has a multitude of stories that they could potentially use in presentations. However, to make them as effective as possible, stories need to be crafted and edited. Stephen King once said, 'When your story is ready for rewrite, cut it to the bone. Get rid of every ounce of excess fat. This is going to hurt, revising a story down to the bare essentials is always a little like murdering children, but it must be done.' This principle also applies to the stories we use in presentations.

The first draft of a story is typically too long, will have sentences that include unnecessary words and a structure that could flow better. It is only by analysing and re-reading the story that it can be edited to convey the message as concisely as possible. To make stories really work, a presenter needs to analyse the structure of the story, the flow of the words, etc. This will help identify the most effective way to deliver the story. I suggest to clients that they type out their stories so that they can see the words on a page. This makes it much easier to see where improvements can be made.

WHY STORIES WORK

Stories work because they make the listener feel. They appeal to the heart as well as to the head.

I believe that stories also work for the following reason. As children most of us went off to sleep at night having been told a bedtime story. The story was the last thing we heard at night so when we fell asleep our subconscious mind replayed the message we received in the format in which it was received. So as children we were trained to process the information we received and trained to receive it in a particular format: a story. It makes sense that having grown up with 'story' as the medium of choice, we still find it to be the preferred method for receiving information and messages.

Let me put it another way. There is no record in history of a child saying to its parents at bedtime, 'Do you know what, tonight I don't want a story. Could I have a PowerPoint presentation instead?'

Stories work because we are comfortable and skilled in telling them. Every day we share our stories and listen to other people's stories. We live stories. We live the experience that the story shares and our audiences do too. We think nothing of telling a story to share our experience or deliver our message.

Stories absolutely meet the four TRUE criteria and are worth 40 points. They have the ability to make audiences think about how your message can benefit or affect them. They certainly make our message easier to remember or recall a day, a week or a month later. Stories create understanding. They allow audiences to make sense of a presenter's message and allow them to do so in their own time. Stories also engage audiences. They draw us into them and leave us wanting to know what is going to happen.

10

THE PRESENTER'S DELIVERY

There are three parts to a great presentation: the content, the structure and the delivery. The delivery of a presentation is a crucial component of an effective presentation. A strong and effective delivery is what engages the audience. As with the content of a presentation, there are things that a presenter can do to increase their engagement with the audience and things that will decrease their chances of getting their message across.

EFFECTIVE PRESENTATION TECHNIQUES
Vocal variety
The voice is the instrument a presenter uses to convey their message, and the way you speak can either enhance or hinder your chances of communicating your message. Used correctly, the voice has the power to persuade and influence the audience. Doing so requires passion and enthusiasm, and these should be reflected in our voice. One way to convey these emotions is through the use of vocal variety.

Vocal variety refers to the pace and volume of the voice. It means speaking faster or more slowly as required to suit the words being said. It means speaking more loudly or softly, again to support the words being used. Vocal variety keeps the audience engaged. Changes in pace and volume signify a change in what is being said and this encourages the audience to listen to what they believe is new or different to what they have been listening to already. Varying the voice in terms of how fast or slow you speak will, when used appropriately, enhance a presenter's ability to connect with their audience. The voice, when varied to support the message being conveyed, will engage an audience and draw them in. It will provide a platform for your audience to follow what you are saying and will make them want to hear more.

When a presenter speaks at a fast pace they convey energy and action. A fast-paced delivery is appropriate to use, for example, if the presenter is speaking about an action-related incident and wants to generate energy and excitement in their audience. An example of a story that would benefit from a fast-paced delivery would be a case where you showed good customer service or problem-solving skills, or had to physically do something to help a client. When relaying the story, the faster pace would support physical actions such as driving to meet the client, picking up a phone to call someone for advice, or even walking from one department to another to get help. The faster pace conveys a sense of urgency that supports the actions being taken to solve the problem.

A slower more deliberate pace conveys less energy, less action and promotes a more serious aspect to a presentation. It is designed to get your audience thinking about what you have said and how it might impact them. It is also designed to help a presenter connect with their audience on an emotional level. Relaying bad news like poor sales figures or financial returns, or announcing job losses would be delivered at a slow pace.

In January 2012 my younger brother, Graham, died suddenly in Australia. I tell the story of Graham's death as part of a larger presentation about the impact we have on the people we meet. My lead-in to Graham's death is delivered at a fast pace, but when I get to the part where Graham dies I slow my pace dramatically. I use the change in pace to create a contrast that highlights this emotional change in the presentation. The following is an extract from that presentation:

Hervey Bay is one of those picture postcard places. Beautiful blue skies, crystal clear water, stunning sandy beaches. It was the furthest point north on my brother Graham's holiday. He was there with his girlfriend, Emily, and her two boys. When they left Hervey Bay, they started the journey back down towards Brisbane. Just outside a little town called Howard, Graham turned to Emily and said, 'I don't feel great.' He pulled the car in at the side of the road. Everyone got out to stretch their legs, get some air. Graham drank some water, took an indigestion tablet, smoked a cigarette and after a few minutes turned to Emily and said, 'I feel much better. We'll be on our way very shortly.' [Everything down to here is delivered at a fast and energetic pace.] *Then, without warning, he dropped to his knees, fell over and was dead before he hit the ground.* [This last sentence is delivered at a much slower pace. After the word 'over' I pause for three to five seconds to add impact and slow the sentence even further.]

Vocal delivery is a skill that requires work and practice if a presenter wants to improve their effectiveness in this area. The majority of presenters could benefit from listening back to how they deliver their own presentations, in order to identify ways to improve their vocal delivery.

I suggest to clients that they should record themselves as they practise delivering sentences from their presentation, with an emphasis on the delivery of those lines. I ask them to deliver the same line a number of different ways with the emphasis on different words in the sentence. I ask them to deliver the line at different paces and degrees of loudness and softness. If the first draft of anything is shit, as Hemingway says, then the first delivery is equally as bad. Have you ever recorded anew the voice message on your mobile phone? Were you happy with the first version you recorded? I will often make ten recordings before I am satisfied.

TRUE Criteria (10 pts)

Good vocal variety meets one of the TRUE criteria. It contributes to engaging the audience and makes a presentation easier to listen to.

Conversational tone

Imagine for a moment you are sitting across a coffee table from your best friend having a catch up. It is a relaxing environment and all you are doing is chatting with your friend. On the way to meet your friend, the thoughts that were going through your mind primarily revolved around what you wanted to talk about, what news you wanted to share. You were not thinking about how to deliver your lines or trying to remember specific words. The result is a relaxed conversation. During it there may have been times when you stumbled over a word or a sentence (you might even have laughed when it happened). There might have been an occasion when you forgot what you were going to say (but that was okay too) and at the end of the chat, when you both got up to leave, you had shared your news in a relaxed manner.

Delivering a presentation should be viewed in exactly the same way. Using a conversational tone adds credibility and believability to the presentation – a conversational tone sounds genuine. It sounds like you want to share a message with your audience without having any other motive than to share something worthwhile.

A conversational style also benefits the presenter. It means you are speaking during a presentation as you normally would; this means it is easier and more natural for the presenter.

I will often advise clients to take time to notice their conversational style, to see how varied their tone is, how animated they might be, how expressive they are, and at other times, how calm. This enables them to become conscious of presenting in the same manner.

TRUE Criteria (10 pts)

A conversational style meets one of the TRUE criteria in that it contributes to engaging an audience. It sounds natural, is easy to listen to and more believable when compared to the forced and unnatural voice presenters sometimes use.

Effective pauses

The ability to 'pause with purpose' is a powerful skill for a presenter to have. It should be straightforward, but some presenters are afraid of the silence that the pause generates. Pauses in a presentation or speech are perfectly acceptable and absolutely essential.

There are a number of reasons for pausing. First, it gives the presenter time to take a breath, which is a necessary requirement for giving a presentation. Second, it can be used to highlight an important part of a sentence. For example, the following sentence would be broken up as follows: 'Stories [pause] are the single most effective element in a presentation [pause] and here's why.' My intention in this sentence is to emphasise the importance of stories. Third, it can be used at the end of a sentence, a paragraph, a story or a question in order to give the audience time to make sense of what you have said or just asked them.

Pauses can be of different lengths depending on their placement or the desired impact. I have witnessed a speech that included an eleven-second pause, and no one in the audience felt it was too long.

I often explain the audience's acceptance of a presenter's pause as follows. Imagine you are in your car and you are stopped at a red light. You are the first car in the queue and for whatever reason you are distracted so that when the light turns green you don't see it immediately. The drivers in the cars behind you now have a choice. Do they beep their horns to encourage you to move or do they wait for you to see the green light yourself? What most drivers do is allow you about three or four seconds before beeping. Audiences will allow a presenter at least the same amount of time.

My suggestion to presenters is to practise their pausing and to include the pauses in their rehearsal. Sometimes, when I have a client who is nervous about pausing, I will encourage them to say '1001, 1002, 1003' in their mind when rehearsing. The presenter would practise as follows. They deliver their sentence, 'Stories are the single most effective element a presenter can use', then pause (1001, 1002, 1003), and then continue speaking. (Don't worry. To date no client of mine has ever said '1001, 1002, 1003' out loud.)

The pause is when the presenter's words begin to make sense. This is when the audience gets time to process and understand them. For this reason, when presenting, the pause can be mightier than the word.

TRUE Criteria (30 pts)

Pauses in presentations meet three of the TRUE criteria in that they allow an audience time to think, create understanding and help to keep an audience engaged.

Confident eye contact

It is said that the three most effective ways to connect with an audience during a presentation are:

1. To tell stories.

2. To effectively use the word 'you' or 'your' to indicate that you are interested in the audience.

3. To make eye contact with your audience.

The third of these can be the most challenging for novice presenters. It can be easier to look at the wall at the back of the room, or even the floor, than at the audience. Most presenters, regardless of how good they are today, will have found making eye contact challenging at some time in their presenting career. It is worth the effort, however, as making eye contact builds trust with members of an audience. Whether presenting to two or three people around a boardroom table, or presenting to a larger group, making eye contact helps a presenter to connect with that audience.

If presenting to a large audience, it is not possible to make eye contact with each individual, so a presenter should mentally divide the audience into a number of different sections and make sure to look at each section during the presentation. A 'section' might contain between ten and twenty people, and when you look at a 'section' many of the ten or twenty people will believe you are looking directly at them.

Eye contact needs to be practised. You don't want to look at an individual audience member for too long, because that person will start to feel uncomfortable, or for too short a time, because you will not connect. Looking at an individual audience member for approximately two seconds is a good place to start. With practice, a presenter will learn to hold the look for longer without scaring the audience member.

As you look around the audience, you will notice different types of attendees. Some attendees will be very supportive. They will smile and nod their heads when the presenter says something they like or agree with. As a presenter it is a good tactic to focus your eye contact on audience members who are supportive. This will strengthen the connection with these members while providing comfort for the presenter.

Equally, there will be some audience members who will not react to what a presenter is saying and who will give the impression of being disinterested in the presentation. There are two things to remember for this sort of person. First, don't become fixated on an audience member who appears not to be enjoying the presentation. Focus on the ones who are. Second, this type of audience member might actually be enjoying your presentation immensely; it just might not be registering in their expression.

TRUE Criteria (10 pts)

Good eye contact meets one of the TRUE criteria. It helps a presenter to connect with members of the audience and keeps them engaged. Good eye contact persuades audience members that your message is directed at them and this helps them to buy into it.

Controlled body language and gestures

There is a story about Victoria Beckham being asked to be a runway model for one of the major fashion designers a number of years ago. She was apparently nervous about doing it and told her mum about her nerves. Her mum's reply is alleged to have been, 'Why are you nervous about walking? You've been doing it since you were two years old.'

The same question could easily be asked about speaking. Why do we get nervous about it when we have been doing it since we were young children? The same thinking also applies to body language. We have conversations every day and never give a moment's thought to what our body is doing. Yet when we stand to speak in front of a group of people, we can become very self-conscious about this.

Rule number one for body language and gestures is that they should never distract. Getting comfortable with body language starts with becoming aware of what you are currently doing and recognising where changes need to be made.

Rule number two: every speaker must be true to themselves. Everyone is different. Some speakers are very energetic and animated with their body language and gestures, while others hardly move at all. One of the best speeches I have ever witnessed was delivered by a ninety-four-year-old man named Joe, who walked up to the stage very slowly, rested his elbow on the lectern to steady himself and never moved from that position throughout his speech. His body language neither supported nor distracted during his speech and as an audience we were mesmerised by his voice, content and message.

Here are my suggestions on the dos and don'ts of using body language during presentations:

1. Video yourself delivering a presentation. Get familiar with how you are using your body and your gestures. You

will see yourself doing things you didn't realise you were doing.

2. Look at other presenters to see what they do well, then select the gestures with which you would be most comfortable. Be prepared to try new actions and movements knowing that they will feel alien to you at the beginning. The purpose of this is to help you add more variety to your movements and ultimately to find the gestures and actions that work for you.

3. Be prepared to evolve. It takes time to find the style that you are comfortable with. It might take years to finally find your true speaking style, but it is worth the effort. One of the challenges that presenters have is what to do with their hands. For a number of years I was unsure what I should do with my hands when not using them to illustrate a point. Initially I would clasp them in front of me like a soccer player standing in the wall for a free kick protecting his prized possessions. Then I started experimenting with different placements, including holding my hands in front me in the steeple position with the tips of my fingers on one hand touching the tips of my fingers on the other. I realised very quickly that this didn't feel natural or look natural to my audience. The change occurred at home one evening. I remember practising a presentation and realising that I was holding my hands differently. I was holding my index finger and middle finger on my left hand (facing

upwards) between the thumb (above) and the index and middle fingers (beneath) on my right hand. I did this unconsciously. It turned out that the most comfortable position for my hands had found me instead of me finding it. That said, I had to go through all the effort of trying other positions before the one that was right for me arrived.

4.   Commit fully to your body language and gestures. In 1986 I was fortunate to be selected to play junior international soccer for the Republic of Ireland. My manager was a guy called Martin Lynch. I always remember something he said during a team talk prior to a match against England: 'Lads, commit to the decision you make. Don't hesitate or doubt your decision. If you make a decision to kick the ball into the stand, stick to it and kick it as far into the stand as possible. If you hesitate or if you start to doubt your decision that is when your opponent will nip in and take the ball from you. That's when a mistake is made.' This is good advice for presenters. Commit fully to your gestures and body language. Confident, committed gestures and strong body language add to a presenter's credibility. They persuade an audience that the presenter is very confident in their message, product, service or idea.

5.   Take a lesson from comedians. When comedians deliver a set they commit 100 per cent to that set. They commit 100 per cent of everything – voice, body, gestures, etc. –

because they know that if their body language and gestures are not fully committed it will have an impact on how the audience reacts, regardless of how good their material is. Good material becomes great material when fully supported by body language and gestures. Comedians are prepared to run the risk of looking foolish in front of an audience because they know that full commitment is required to generate the reaction they are looking for in their audience.

6. Don't be too quick to return your arm to the neutral position after you have used it to point or gesture. For example, you might use your arm to point at something on your PowerPoint slide. When you do, don't return your arm to the neutral position – which is usually down by your side – too quickly. Be prepared to hold your arm in the pointing position a little longer. If you return your arm to the neutral position too quickly the whole gesture will feel rushed. Recording how you use gestures will tell you if you are returning your arm to the neutral position too quickly.

7. Practice, practice, practice. There is no substitute for practice. This can be done in private. Video record five minutes of a speech or presentation and look at what your body and gestures are doing. Identify what is working and keep doing it. Identify what needs to be improved and practise and record the improvements until you are happy with them.

TRUE Criteria (10 pts)

Controlled body language and gestures meet one of the TRUE criteria in that they engage the audience and avoid being a distraction.

INEFFECTIVE PRESENTATION TECHNIQUES

Monotone voice

The voice attracts the ear in the same way that movement attracts the eye. A voice that is monotonous has no movement and after a while struggles to attract the ear. If a presenter delivers a presentation in a monotone voice an audience will get bored with it very quickly. Monotonous voices don't reflect the emotions we want audiences to feel during a presentation. They lack the contrast that lets the audience know when something is changing in the presentation and fail to generate excitement in the audience to keep them listening.

TRUE Criteria (-40 pts)

A monotonous voice meets none of the TRUE criteria. It has the potential to cause an audience to become bored and stop listening.

Formal tone

On occasions presenters develop a 'formal tone' when delivering a presentation. A presenter who uses a formal tone will pronounce every single word in a very deliberate and complete manner. The presenter will use words like 'could not' or 'would not' when in real life we would say 'wouldn't' or 'couldn't'.

Sometimes a presenter uses a formal tone deliberately and sometimes it is by accident, as a way to protect themselves when speaking in front of an audience. I believe that some presenters think that a formal tone makes them sound more credible or more in control.

However, given that a formal tone is not a natural way to speak in everyday conversation, using it in a presentation has the potential to create a barrier between the presenter and an audience. This means it has the potential to hinder the presenter's chances of getting their message across.

TRUE Criteria (-40 pts)

A formal tone meets none of the TRUE criteria. In fact, it has the potential to hinder audience engagement, which makes a message more difficult to remember and understand, and stops an audience from thinking about the message the presenter is trying to get across.

One-dimensional pace

A presenter who delivers a presentation at the same pace the whole way through runs the risk of losing their audience and not getting their message across. Not all parts of a presentation are of equal importance. Some parts of a presentation are just the set-up for the more important parts. When a presentation is delivered at the same pace throughout, it becomes difficult for the audience to distinguish what is more important and what is worth remembering. The danger with one-dimensional pacing is that it makes an audience work harder than they should have to and audiences that are forced to work hard usually stop working altogether.

TRUE Criteria (-40 pts)

A one-dimensional pace fails to meet any of the TRUE criteria as it stops an audience from engaging with the presentation and makes it more difficult to remember and understand the message being delivered.

Lack of pauses

A presenter who doesn't take time to pause runs the risk of alienating the audience. Delivering a presentation without pauses makes it more difficult for your audience to keep up with what you are saying. Throughout a presentation there are times when your audience needs time to digest and make sense of something you have said. Pausing allows them to do that. When a presenter doesn't include pauses in the presentation it causes a problem for the audience and forces them to make a choice. Do they stop listening to the presenter to make sense of the previous thing the presenter has said, or do they forget about digesting that point and carry on listening to the presenter? When given a choice like this, audiences will often take a third option – stop listening altogether.

TRUE Criteria (-40 pts)

Lack of pauses meets none of the TRUE criteria. The lack of a pause gives your audience an excuse to stop engaging with your message. It makes it harder to make sense of what a presenter has said and hinders understanding. It allows your audience to stop thinking about your message because they are not being given time to think.

Lack of eye contact

Failing to make eye contact can cause audiences to doubt a presenter or their message. A lack of eye contact can also result in a lack of trust of the presenter. Audiences can potentially believe that the reason the presenter won't make eye contact is because their message is not trustworthy or that they themselves aren't convinced by their message. Audiences who don't trust a presenter won't buy into their message.

For most presenters, a lack of eye contact is usually something they encounter at the start of a presenting career. It often stems from being nervous. They find it easier to look at the wall at the back of the room or at their slides or at the floor.

If you are aware of a need to make better eye contact my suggestion is to start slow. Don't try to get to everybody at once. Select one or two members of the audience and start by making eye contact with them. With each future presentation aim to look at a couple more people. Over time it will become easier to make eye contact with as many audience members as possible.

TRUE Criteria (-40 pts)

A lack of eye contact meets none of the TRUE criteria. It causes an audience to mistrust a presenter and their message. Audiences believe there must be a reason why the presenter can't look them in the eye.

Uncomfortable body language and gestures

A presenter who appears uncomfortable when presenting reduces their credibility and impacts negatively on their message. Audiences buy into the presenter as much as the message. If a presenter is unsure of their movements or gestures, then the audience can become distracted because the presenter appears unnatural or uncommitted. This in turn leads an audience to find a presenter unconvincing and they won't buy into that presenter's message.

Uncomfortable body language is usually due to inexperience or nerves. Again, recording how you use your body or apply gestures will help you to identify areas on which to work.

TRUE Criteria (-40 pts)

Uncomfortable body language and gestures meet none of the TRUE criteria. They can be distracting and cause an audience to think that the presenter's message is unconvincing.

NOTE

I want to add one caveat to this chapter on delivery. Great delivery is important but it will not compensate for poor content and structure. I say this because, down through the years, I have witnessed many presentations, delivered with confidence and composure by sales professionals, which lacked content and structure and so ultimately failed to meet the TRUE criteria and, more importantly, failed to influence their audience.

PRESENTATION SCORECARD			
Presenter's Delivery	**Points**	**TRUE Criteria**	**My Score**
Vocal variety	10	E	
Conversational tone	10	E	
Effective pauses	30	TEU	
Confident eye contact	10	E	
Controlled body language and gestures	10	E	
Monotone voice	-40		
Formal tone	-40		
One-dimensional pace	-40		
Lack of pauses	-40		
Lack of eye contact	-40		
Uncomfortable body language and gestures	-40		

11

CLOSING YOUR PRESENTATION

I mentioned in Chapter 4 that, as per the 1978 Hartley and Davies study, audiences are at their most attentive at the beginning and end of a presentation. Therefore it makes sense that at the end of a presentation, when the audience is listening most attentively, a presenter should be saying something worth hearing. Too often presenters miss the opportunity to reinforce their message.

The following are some dos and don'ts.

HOW TO END A PRESENTATION WELL

Call to action

There is huge value in telling your audience what you want them to do at the end of your presentation. Sometimes that's just what they need. Ending on a call to action removes doubt in their mind. They may not act on it but at least they will know what you want them to do. An example of a call to action is to use a simple phrase such as, 'So if this presentation has made sense, the next step is …' or 'If you would like to act on this, there is no better time than right now.' At the end of the presentation that I deliver on TRUE presentations, I will often finish as follows: 'So if this presentation has made sense, and you think it would be of interest to other people in your organisation, or if you would like to know more, come and see me afterwards or give me a call. My number is …'

TRUE Criteria (30 pts)

A call to action meets three of the TRUE criteria. It will make your audience think, will generate understanding of the message you want them to act upon and will engage them because you have given them something to consider.

A story

A great way to finish your presentation is with a story, particularly a story which has a message that is self-explanatory and doesn't require clarification. I am a huge fan of finishing a presentation with a story that supports the message I want to get across and then leaving it hanging there so that the audience reaches 'my' conclusion by themselves. There is the added benefit of giving your audience an emotional hit at the end of the presentation that will make your ending and message even easier to remember.

Here is a story relating to TRUE presentations that I often use to finish: 'Ladies and gentlemen, I would like to finish with this. A couple of years ago, I was contacted by Dermot. At the time he was the business development manager for a software company and wanted help with a presentation he was going to be delivering to a potential client. At the outset he told me that his company were not expected to win the business but that they wanted to be able to give a good account of themselves.

'Dermot agreed to allow me to take him through the TRUE process from the beginning. It took a bit of time but eventually we had constructed what I considered to be a strong and persuasive presentation. Dermot spent time getting comfortable delivering it and eventually the time came to deliver it to the potential client. He phoned me the day after to say that the presentation had gone very well and that the client had appreciated and enjoyed its innovative nature. A month later he phoned to tell me that his company had won the contract and that the client had told them that the presentation had contributed to the decision. The contract is worth €1,000,000 over five years. When I get asked if TRUE presentations can help sales teams, this is the story I tell.'

TRUE Criteria (40 pts)

Stories meet the four TRUE criteria. They influence the audience's thinking, aid recall, create understanding and help engage the audience.

Recap of outcomes

Another good way to finish a presentation is with a recap of the outcomes the audience can expect to receive from buying into your message. Finish by extolling the benefits of your presentation's message. The added benefit is that, stated at the end of the presentation, these outcomes will be the last words your audience hears, which will make them more memorable.

For example, I worked with a client some time ago who came to me with an existing presentation. It was a typical 'this is who we are, this is what we do' presentation. I persuaded them to change it so that it reflected the benefits to their potential client of working with them. I encouraged them to close their presentation with a recap of those benefits as follows. 'I would like to leave you with this. We believe that we can help you to reduce your costs, save time, increase your bottom-line profitability and further enhance your existing reputation, and that is why we ask you to consider us as one of your gold standard partners.'

TRUE Criteria (30 pts)

Recapping the key outcomes from your presentation meets three of the TRUE criteria. Recapping the benefits to your audience will reinforce why they should take the action you want them to take. It makes them think, can aid recall because they are hearing the same message repeated and repeating it will also allow for further understanding.

Scripted closing comments

The words you use at the end of your presentation will be delivered at the point when your audience are at or near their most attentive. These words could well be the easiest words they can remember a day, a week or a month later so, in my opinion, a presenter has an obligation to make sure they are as well-crafted as possible. This is not the time to speak off the cuff or ramble. You are going to leave them with a clear picture of what you want them to do and that means scripting what you are going to say. In Chapter 13 I will talk about crafting the words. For now, let's just say that I have yet to meet anyone who can craft the best and most effective words the first time, every time.

While a presenter might use key phrases to help them plot

their way through the body of the presentation, the opening and the closing need to be scripted. This means writing out your ending, then rewriting and rewriting until you have the clearest message in the fewest words. A carefully considered and well-scripted closing will have a far greater impact than one that is not.

TRUE Criteria (30 pts)

Scripting your closing comments meets three of the TRUE criteria. It will make the audience think and promotes a clearer understanding of what you want them to do next. It will keep them engaged because your closing will be short and clear, allowing them to get your message with the smallest amount of effort.

HOW TO END A PRESENTATION BADLY

Closing on questions

There is an expectation that presentations should finish with a questions and answers section. The danger with this is twofold:

1. It can dilute the presenter's message because the audience are not thinking about what the presenter wants them thinking about.

2. It impacts on a presenter's credibility if they are asked a question they cannot answer with confidence and composure.

If a presenter has to finish on questions – and sometimes they won't have a choice – then the way around this is to include (after the questions have been asked) a final quote, question or sentence that supports the message the presenter wants the audience to take away and make it the last thing they hear.

When I deliver my presentation on TRUE presentations I will sometimes finish up by asking the audience four questions as follows: 'Right, if that is all the questions, let me ask you, has what I spoke about today contributed to your **thinking**? A week from now do you think it will be easy enough to **recall** some of the things I have said today? Was what I spoke about today easy to **understand**? Was it **engaging**?' I ask the audience to answer each question. They always answer 'yes'. The purpose of this is to allow me to reinforce the TRUE message.

TRUE Criteria (-40 pts)

Closing on audience questions meets none of the TRUE criteria. Finishing a presentation like this can dilute the presenter's message and has the potential to impact negatively on their credibility and composure, which might convince an audience not to buy into their message.

The 'Thank You' slide

So many presenters finish their presentation with a PowerPoint slide that simply says 'Thank You'. They therefore miss a great opportunity to reinforce the message they want their audience to take away and act on.

Saying 'thank you' to an audience is the presenter's job.

Putting it onto a slide is lazy. There are three problems with the 'Thank You' slide. First, saying thank you would be much more genuine and more appreciated by the audience if delivered by a presenter without a prompt from technology. Second, it misses an opportunity to end by driving home the presenter's message. Imagine if the 'Thank You' slide was replaced by a slide that reinforces the message the presenter wants to get across. When speaking about TRUE presentations, my final slide will say:

TRUE Presentations –

Helping you to create clear compelling presentations that win business

Seeing that message visually can help to reinforce it and make it easier to remember.

Finally, finishing on 'Thank You' potentially suggests to the audience that you don't require them to take action at the end of your presentation. A sales presentation is not a stand-alone event. It is one part of the process of getting your client or prospect to buy into your idea, service or product. Therefore, a presenter should be finishing with a call to action.

TRUE Criteria (-40 pts)

Finishing a presentation with a 'Thank You' slide misses an opportunity to reinforce, visually, the message you want your audience to take away and act on. It implies that you have reached the end of your presentation and no more action is required. It potentially gives an audience an excuse to do nothing further.

PRESENTATION SCORECARD			
Presentation Close	**Points**	**TRUE Criteria**	**My Score**
Call to action	30	TUE	
A story	40	TRUE	
Recap of outcomes	30	TRU	
Scripted closing comments	30	TUE	
Close on questions	-40		
The 'Thank You' slide	-40		

12

USING POWERPOINT SLIDES

PowerPoint slides are a great presentation support tool, but today they only seem to receive bad press. This bad press is reinforced by phrases such as 'Death by PowerPoint', the inference being that the PowerPoint slides have been responsible for ruining a presentation and the audience's enjoyment of said presentation. A more accurate phrase would be: 'Death by presenter using PowerPoint poorly'. If a presentation is poor, it is the presenter's fault. If the PowerPoint slides are poor, it is still the presenter's fault.

I believe that PowerPoint is used poorly for a number of reasons. First, most presenters don't have the time to learn fully what PowerPoint is capable of and, second, they often don't have enough time to prepare their presentations and, as a consequence, take the easy option regarding slides and load them with text.

Used properly PowerPoint can be a wonderful visual aid to a presentation. I have deliberately used the words 'visual aid', because that's what the slides should be used for – to provide a visual stimulus. They should be used to support the presenter.

My view of PowerPoint is that it should enhance a presentation without becoming its centrepiece. If the slides are not going to enhance the presentation the presenter should not use them. A good presenter should be able to deliver a presentation without slides, if for no other reason than someday the technology won't work and they will need to be able to get their message across regardless.

HOW TO MAKE EFFECTIVE POWERPOINT SLIDES
Balance of words and pictures

Presenters have three options with slides if they choose to use them:

1. The slides can contain words only, often in the form of bullet points.

2. They can have pictures only (this can include graphs).

3. They can have pictures and words.

Personally, I believe that slides that have both pictures and words are the most effective. Pictures create a great visual support for the words and message that the presenter is sharing. However, if used alone, pictures are open to interpretation. It is possible for members of your audience to see an image on a slide and have it mean something to them other than the message you are looking to get across. When a presenter uses an image on a slide and supports it with a small number of words, it gives the presenter the best chance of getting their message across and having it remembered.

Opposite is an example of a slide I used a couple of years ago to illustrate kinaesthetic engagement. In presentation terms kinaesthetic engagement refers to getting your audience to do something physically, and often that action is with their hands. (If I was using a slide to illustrate visual engagement, the image would be an eye, or, if illustrating auditory engagement, the image would be an ear.) This slide shows a strong image that engages an audience. The word on the slide guides the audience to what I am talking about, but in order to understand the message they then have to listen to me.

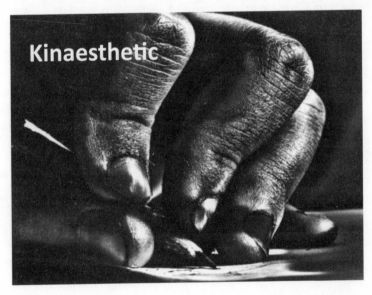

(© Louise Fitzpatrick)

TRUE Criteria (20 pts)

Slides containing words and pictures meet two of the TRUE criteria. They help to engage your audience and create understanding.

Slides are for the audience

Your slides should be created with your audience in mind. They should be created to help them understand your message or to generate engagement. I have, when appropriate, created slides whose sole purpose was to generate laughter among the audience because I knew it would keep them engaged.

When preparing a slide, I ask myself what my audience needs to read or see on the slide. What does the slide require to help get the message across? Seeing the presentation from their perspective allows me to tailor the slides to meet their needs. This might, for example, mean changing the words on the slides so that they are 'them' focused, or highlighting the benefits rather than the features of a product.

Opposite is an example of a slide I used a few years ago during a workshop on humour. I was giving an example of the 'mindreading' technique described in Chapter 8. Its purpose was to generate laughter and to engage my audience. When I brought up the slide initially it only contained the words 'Catherine and I have been married for 23 years'. I then suggested that based upon that statement they were now thinking one of the following three things. I animated the slide so that each point appeared on the slide separately.[1] Most

---

1 PowerPoint slides can be set up so that the information on them doesn't appear on the slide all together. 'Animating' the slides means setting up the slide so that different pieces of information appear when the presenter wants them to. For example, if you had a slide with six bullet points on it and they all appear on the slide in one go, this causes a problem for a presenter because the audience will read faster than the presenter can speak and they will read all the bullet points that the presenter hasn't yet reached. Animating the slide means a presenter can bring one bullet point up at a time, which means the audience has to focus on the point the

of the audience that day had selected option number three, which I believed they would. This slide engaged the audience for two reasons: firstly, because they had to think about their answer, and secondly, because their answer was on the slide. They appreciated the fact that I had taken the time to consider how they would react in this instance.

Catherine and I have been married for 23 years

1. Congratulations

2. You don't look old enough

3. The Poor Girl!!!

TRUE Criteria (40 pts)

Slides that are built for the audience meet the four TRUE criteria. They get them thinking, generate understanding, aid recall and keep them engaged.

Slides are easy to follow

Don't make your slides too difficult to follow. Don't make your audience work any harder than they have to. You want your audience to understand your message, not spend time trying to work out the message you are trying to get across. Slides

---

presenter is speaking about and can't get distracted by other information on the slide.

that are easy to follow allow your audience to focus on your message. The best ways to make your slides easy to follow are:

1. Keep the information to a minimum.

2. Don't use language or industry jargon that isn't familiar to your audience.

3. Structure the content so that it is easy to navigate.

TRUE Criteria (10 pts)

Slides that are easy to follow meet one of the TRUE criteria. They make it easier for your audience to understand your message.

Uniform slides

Slides should look consistent. If you build slides around pictures, then pictures should be included on every slide. Your slides should have a uniformity in appearance as your presentation progresses. This will allow your audience to focus on your message and not become distracted by the slides. Slides that are not alike cause audiences to switch their focus from the message to the slide, but the slides themselves should never be the centre of attention.

TRUE Criteria (10 pts)

Slides that are uniform meet one of the TRUE criteria. They help to create understanding.

Slides are built around the presentation

Slides should be built only after the presentation's objective, message and content have been decided upon. Slides should be the last thing the presenter works on. This enables them to be a supporting act to the presenter and the message. The advantages of creating slides last are:

1. You are not dependent on them.

2. The slides need less content because you are more familiar with your message.

3. The slides support the message you want your audience to take away.

Building the slides around your presentation also means that you can create slides that, on their own, don't tell the whole story, which means that the audience have to listen to the presenter if they are going to get the message.

TRUE Criteria (30 pts)

Slides that are built around the presentation meet three of the TRUE criteria. They encourage the audience to think about your message and not reach their own conclusion, and help create understanding and engagement because they need to listen to you to fully understand the message.

No slides

Sometimes presentations are delivered without slides (I know, the horror). This is because the presenter makes a deliberate decision not to use them or because the technology doesn't work (and, on occasions, it won't). There are benefits to delivering a presentation 'unplugged'. For example, your audience has to focus on you. You are not competing for your audience's attention with your slides. Furthermore, the fact that they don't have to rely on slides can enhance the reputation of a presenter and, lastly, there is less that can go wrong when you are slide-free (sometimes the technology can fail in the middle of the presentation).

I often deliver presentations without slides for two reasons. First, I want the delivery of my message to be the driver in persuading my audience. When we deliver presentations we are being judged on who we are and how we come across just as much as we are being judged on our message. A prospective client might like the message, but if they don't like the presenter they will not buy. Second, sometimes (in my opinion) slides get in the way. Slides fix the journey the presenter must take through their message and I find this restrictive. I like to keep my audience involved throughout my presentation and that means going off script on occasion in order to react to a question or comment from the audience. It means going off script when a story I haven't planned on using is suddenly very suitable to use because of something the audience has said. Slides make 'going off script' harder to do.

It is worth considering that in a world where slides are

the norm, delivering a presentation without them can make a presenter stand out from their competition, whether that is pitching to win a client contract or investor funding. In all the times I have delivered a presentation without slides no one has ever come up to me and suggested that my presentation would have been better if slides had been used. There is also an incorrect perception that a presentation where slides are used is somehow more professional. This is not the case. Some of the best presentations ever have been delivered free of slides.

TRUE Criteria (10 pts)

Presenting without slides meets one of the TRUE criteria. It gives you the opportunity to strengthen your engagement with your audience – there is just you and them. Some audiences will admire you more for not using (relying on) slides and that will encourage them to connect with you and your message.

Slides do not distract

Slides are there to support the message you want to get across. They should not become the focus of your audience's attention. At the end of the presentation your audience should not be talking about your slides but about your message. It is a bit like the referee in a football match. They should never be the centre of attention. They should contribute to our enjoyment of the game, not be our focus at the end of it. Likewise slides should contribute to both our enjoyment of the presentation and to our receipt of the message.

TRUE Criteria (10 pts)

Slides that do not distract aid our understanding of the message.

WHAT NOT TO DO

Text-heavy slides

Presenters often put lots of text onto their slides. This is a bad idea for a number of reasons:

1. Your audience can read so they don't need to listen to you.

2. Your audience will read faster than you speak so they will have reached the end of the text on the slide before you do and will start to form their own opinions. This is hugely detrimental to getting your message across.

3. If you need to read from your slides this means turning your back on your audience. They will find this disrespectful, which will make it less likely that they will buy into your message.

4. Slides that are full of text miss the opportunity to visually stimulate their audience. This means that you miss the opportunity to reinforce your message by connecting with more than one of the senses.

Opposite is a slide I used in a presentation about eleven years ago. It has too much text on it. It is really more of a document than a visual aid. Ironically, some of the points being made on the slide about PowerPoint presentations actually highlight many of the things that are wrong with it.

TOO MANY WORDS

- There are different ways to use PowerPoint. Some are more effective than others.
- Use different font sizes for the heading than for the text. For the heading use a minimum of 40. For the text use a minimum of 32.
- Don't give your audience an eye exam. If the text is too small or there are too many words the audience will not be able to read it and lose interest in listening to you as well.
- The six by six rule is a very useful guide for using PowerPoint effectively.
- Remember PowerPoint is only an aid. It is there to support you, not to replace you or be used in place of you.
- Don't be too clever with PowerPoint. There are all sorts of ways to make Power Point more interesting, just make sure they are not a distraction.
- Don't be too dull with PowerPoint. If used well it can be a valuable addition to your presentation.

TRUE Criteria (-40 pts)

Slides with too much text meet none of the TRUE criteria. They run the risk of having your audience think about something other than the message you want them to get. They reduce engagement and make your message harder to understand.

Slides are for the presenter

Presenters will often use their slides as their own notes. They use them to help them remember what they want to say. This is not a good use of slides. Much like putting too much text on the slides, creating slides for yourself and not for your audience will harm the impact of your presentation. Your audience want to believe that you have taken the time to prepare sufficiently for your presentation. Using slides to help you remember tells your audience that you haven't and this will hinder the connection with them.

Here is an example of a slide I created whose sole purpose was to help me to remember what I wanted to talk about. It is too text heavy and caused my audience to read the slide rather than listen to me.

PLANNING & PREPARATION

1. PLAN YEAR: No. of working days. All of our monthly offers. Areas to focus on i.e. Products, Customers, Brands, Sales Target.

2. PLAN MONTH: Who I will visit. When I will visit (which week). Why I will visit.

3. PLAN WEEK: As 'Plan Month'

4. PLAN DAY: I prepare all I have to do for each day the night before. Who I will visit. Why I am visiting. How much time I will spend at each call. What cold calls I will make if I have any time to spare. Review all calls made and implement follow-up action to be taken.

TRUE Criteria (-40 pts)

Creating slides that are for the presenter meets none of the TRUE criteria. It gives your audience the opportunity to think about you in a negative way and not about your message. Slides created for the presenter do nothing to promote understanding, and they break the connection with the audience when you turn to look at the screen, which will hinder the audience's engagement.

Slides contain industry jargon

Giving a presentation can be a nerve-racking experience and it is natural for presenters to try to protect themselves when they are in this spotlight. One way presenters protect themselves is by trying to sound as knowledgeable as possible. They do this by using industry terms and jargon. The use of terms that an audience is not familiar with may make a presenter sound like an expert, but if the audience is not familiar with those terms they will not care that the presenter is so knowledgeable because they won't be listening any more. Nothing turns an audience off like not understanding what the presenter is talking about. Even on occasions where you are presenting to members of your own industry, who are familiar with the industry terms, this jargon-heavy approach is still not recommended. This applies just as much to your slides as it does to your presentation.

Remember that the objective of your presentation is to get across your message. Our words are the tools we use to achieve this, so keep them as simple as possible. I regularly deliver presentation training to very clever scientists at the Tyndall Research Institute in County Cork, Ireland. During the training, I will often remind them that I am the dumbest guy in the room and give them the task of delivering a presentation on their topic in language that I will understand. Some of them speak in terms that fly so far over my head I have switched off within the first few seconds. Others, however, recognise the merit in speaking in words that make sense to me – they see the inherent clarity of such an approach – and create a presentation that non-scientific audiences would easily understand. From a presentation perspective, the less jargon a presenter uses in their words and on their slides, the easier it will be to get their message across.

TRUE Criteria (-40 pts)

Using industry jargon meets none of the TRUE criteria. It runs the risk of hindering understanding of your message and if your audience doesn't understand what you are saying they won't get your message.

Detail-heavy slides

Slides need to be kept as simple as possible. The more you put into a slide the harder you make your audience work and audiences don't like that. This can mean having too many images on the same slide. It can mean having too many concepts. It is better to have more slides with less information on each, than to have fewer slides that no one is paying attention to because they are too difficult to follow. One idea per slide is a good rule of thumb.

Opposite I have provided an example of a slide with too much detail. Excluding the title and subtitle, there are seven different pieces of information on this slide. The audience's eye is drawn to too many different places, which dilutes the message being shared. Also, you will notice that sections of this slide are very poorly worded. The first part on the right, which starts with the words '50 Hours', is potentially confusing to my audience. My intention in this part was to state that I had stopped carrying out an activity (visiting the bank) that used to take one hour per week to complete. In a single year that equated to 50 hours visiting the bank, which is the equivalent of one working week. Having stopped visiting the bank I had created an extra week's time to focus on selling. However, worded as it is below, my audience probably spent more time trying to work out what I was attempting to convey than listening to my message.

TIME MANAGEMENT
CREATING MORE SELLING TIME

- Eliminate visit to the Bank to lodge cheques.

- Using lunchtime constructively.

- Starting earlier, finishing later.

- 50 hours (1 visit per week took 1 hour) in 2003 spent visiting bank. The equivalent of 1 full working week - this year spent selling.

- 1 hour per day = 5 hours per week = 250 hours per year = 6 x 40 hour weeks. We spent this time working & eating.

- Using time that could not be spent in front of customers doing quotes, returns, credits, assessing accounts.

12 weeks of time created to spend on selling

TRUE Criteria (-40 pts)

Slides with too much detail meet none of the TRUE criteria. They hinder understanding of your message and cause audiences to become disengaged from your presentation.

Presentation built around slides

Slides are the starting point for many presenters. They begin the process of preparing a presentation by creating slides as they go along (or by using the slides from a previous presentation). They will decide on a piece of information they would like to include in their presentation and build a slide to support (or help themselves to remember) that point.

This is dangerous for a number of reasons. Presenters need to see the overall picture before they start creating their slides. They can't do that if they focus on building slides as they go. Moreover, building the presentation around the slides makes them the centrepiece of the presentation. This means that the message needs to fit with the slides when it should be the other way around. The message should come first and the slides should be the last thing created.

Presentations built around slides create a couple of problems: firstly, the presenter is now dependent on the slides and, secondly, as the centrepiece of the presentation, there is a greater chance that audiences will look at them instead of listening to the presenter.

TRUE Criteria (-40 pts)

Presentations built around slides meet none of the TRUE

criteria. This can hinder understanding (audiences might get a different message to the one you want them to take away) and engagement (audiences might form their own opinion based on the slides and not on what you say, and could potentially switch off from listening to you). They can also make your message harder to recall.

Slides are too technical

PowerPoint slides have many features that can potentially make them more exciting to look at. They can be made to appear on the screen in a variety of ways, from fading in slowly, to appearing from the left or the right, to floating upwards from the bottom of the screen. The words on the slide can be made to appear by entering from the left of the slide or can arrive onto the slide spinning furiously. Sometimes presenters get wrapped up in making their slides exciting at the expense of their message. Presenters who focus too much on the technical capability of PowerPoint run the risk of losing their audience. The novelty of a fancily delivered slide or set of words on a slide wears off very quickly. Instead such effects are a distraction which detract from the message.

TRUE Criteria (-40 pts)

Slides that are too technical meet none of the TRUE criteria.

PRESENTATION SCORECARD			
PowerPoint Slides	**Points**	**TRUE Criteria**	**My Score**
Balance of words and pictures	20	UE	
Slides are for the audience	40	TRUE	
Slides are easy to follow	10	U	
Slides are uniform	10	U	
Slides are built around the presentation	30	TUE	
No slides used	10	E	
Slides do not distract	10	U	
Text-heavy slides	-40		
Slides are for the presenter	-40		
Slides contain industry jargon	-40		
Detail-heavy slides	-40		
Presentation built around the slides	-40		
Slides are too technical	-40		

13

CRAFTING YOUR PRESENTATION

As previously noted, Mark Twain once said, 'The difference between the almost right word and the right word is really a large matter – 'tis the difference between the lightning-bug and the lightning.' There is huge merit in taking the time to carefully craft the wording of your presentation. Anything that helps bring clarity to your message and makes it easier to understand is worth spending time on.

In my opinion, every word of a presentation should be carefully considered. It takes time, patience and effort. The best presentation is not written in the back of a taxi on the way to delivering it. It requires making mistakes and learning from them. It requires taking your ego out of the equation and getting input from people who have no emotional attachment to the presentation. It requires a lot of things that many presenters are not prepared to give. That said, for the presenters who are prepared to put this time and effort in, the reward is well worth it. They end up with presentations that have a clear, concise message and give themselves the best opportunity to influence their audience.

REWRITE, REWRITE, REWRITE

As I mentioned earlier in the book, the first draft of anything is never perfect and this is especially true of presentations. Your first attempt at a presentation will never be your best attempt. No one gets the words right the first time. Some of the best presentations have been rewritten multiple times until they are as good as the presenter is capable of making them.

In 2010 I gave a speech that was rewritten twenty-three times. (Just to be clear, the entire speech wasn't rewritten each time. I would change the order of sentences, change the order of words in sentences and change words in sentences. Each rewrite was smaller than the previous one. Changing the speech from the twenty-second to the twenty-third rewrite only involved changing a couple of words.) One of the lines in that speech generated a huge amount of laughter from the audience and was referenced by a number of people a couple of years later. This line wasn't in the first five drafts of my speech. I would have missed a golden opportunity to connect with my audience if I hadn't been open to the idea of working to improve my speech. The process of rewriting a speech or presentation means that, as a presenter, you are open to receiving new ideas that could enhance your message.

EDITING SENTENCES

Speaking coach Patricia Fripp talks about the importance of constructing sentences in a way that allows them to have the greatest impact. She talks about the idea that, in sentences, some words are more important than others and about the importance of creating sentences that have rhythm and flow.

For me there are four elements to a good sentence. First, there is the beginning of the sentence. This is where the least important information in the sentence is placed. Second, there is the order of the words in the sentence. (I know that sounds strange but bear with me.) Third, there is the end of the sentence. This is about making sure that the sentence finishes on the key word. Fourth, there are the words themselves. When it comes to the words themselves, the smaller the better. As I've discussed earlier, fancier words are not the way to go. Use words that the audience can clearly understand.

Comedians will often talk about how they construct their jokes and the different parts to them. Each joke should have a set-up and a punchline. The punchline should finish on the punch word. Finally, the comedian aims to deliver the joke in the fewest words possible. A good example of this is the following joke from Canadian comedian Stewart Francis: 'I saw a documentary about how ships are kept together. It was riveting.' The set-up is: 'I saw a documentary about how ships are kept together.' The punchline is: 'It was riveting.' The punch word is 'riveting'. There are thirteen words in total and the joke benefits from finishing on the word 'riveting'. This is the word that generates the laughter. The joke could have been written as follows, but wouldn't have been as effective: 'I watched a programme on TV last night about how ships are made. It was a riveting documentary.' The joke now contains eighteen words and finishes on the wrong word. In this version the word 'documentary' steps on the laughter because it comes after the word that makes us laugh.

As presenters we should be aiming for the same with every sentence. Taking the time and effort to construct our sentences as carefully as possible gives presenters the best chance to influence their audience.

Now let's have a look at a very simple sentence constructed in a number of different ways:

1. In order to deliver training, speaking and coaching services, in 2009 I set up my business.

2. I set up my business to deliver training, speaking and coaching services in 2009.

3. In 2009 I set up my business to deliver training, speaking and coaching services.

In the first example, by finishing on the words 'set up my business', I am suggesting that setting up my business is the important part of this sentence. By finishing on the words 'in 2009' in the second example I am suggesting that the year I set up the business is the most important part of this sentence. In the third example, by finishing on the words 'training, speaking and coaching services', I am suggesting that the services I offer within my business are the most important part of this sentence.

The third example is the way I would construct this sentence almost every time. The year I set up my business is not the most important piece of information I want to share. Talking about my business is not the most important piece of information either. The piece of information I want an audience to hear in that sentence is that I offer training, speaking and coaching services.

SPEAK FIRST, WRITE SECOND

I believe that in order to craft the most effective presentation possible you have to write out your presentation word-for-word. Let me say that I know this is not always possible. Let me also say that sometimes presenters won't bother because it seems too much like hard work. That said, where it is possible, and where a presenter is inclined to put in the effort, there are big rewards available. The flow and rhythm of the words of a presentation are easier to see in written form and are therefore easier to change. (Writing this book has driven this home to me. There have been numerous times when I have written a sentence, paragraph or chapter and upon rereading it a couple of days later have found better ways to get my message across.)

Most people agree that the written word is different to the spoken word, so the key, from the point of view of the presentation, is initially to speak the words you want to say aloud and then put those words onto paper. Don't write first and hope to speak those words. Do it in reverse. Speak first. Write second. This is useful for a number of reasons. For example, we speak in abbreviations, saying things like 'I can't' or 'I wouldn't'. When writing we would write 'I cannot' or 'I would not'. When writing out the words of the presentation, it is recommended that you use the abbreviated versions. This will sound more natural when speaking to your audience.

14

BRINGING IT ALL TOGETHER: THE PRESENTATION TEMPLATE

I have covered a lot of ground in the previous thirteen chapters. You will now be aware of the elements that help and hinder presenters as they attempt to convey their message to an audience. This chapter is about bringing it all together, particularly in terms of creating the presentation that you would want to give, that an audience will want to sit through, and that will allow you to get your message across in a way that will encourage your audience to buy into it.

This chapter provides you with a template for creating impactful presentations. I call it the 'TRUE Presentation Template'. This template includes only the elements that will help you get your message across. These are the elements I encourage you to consider using from now on. I know this will be difficult to begin with as it will be strange not to use elements that so many other presenters currently utilise and that you perhaps use yourself. Remember this: one of the things that will make your presentation stand out is being different from all the other 'typical' presentations.

Another advantage of the template is that, as you become familiar with it, it will help reduce the amount of time you spend creating your presentations (without compromising on quality).

The "TRUE Presentation" Template by ARK Speaking and Training

Pre-Presentation		
What is my objective?		
Who is my audience and how will they benefit?		
Brainstorm		

Presentation Opening		Engagement
A Story		
A Quotation		
A Challenge		
An Interesting Statistic		
A Question		
State your outcomes		
Humour		
Reference what is on mind of the audience		
Get audience to do something		Humour
Reference something mentioned earlier		
Opening is scripted		Story
Agenda		
Outline of Presentation including duration		Dialogue

Message	Roadmap	Engagement
Message		Questions
	Opening/Middle/End	
		Audience Involvement
Key Point 1	Numerical	
		Rhetorical Devices
	Chronological	
Key Point 2		Visual Engagement
	Situation/Solution	
		Auditory Engagement
Key Point 3	Rhetorical Question	
		Kinaesthetic Engagement
	Features/Benefits	
Key Point 4		Props
	Case Study	
		"Them" Focused
Key point 5	Modular	
		Concrete Images
Q&A		Emotional Connection
Presentation Close		Quotations
Call to Action		
Recall Key Benefits		
Story		
Question		
Closing is scripted		

Finally the template is deliberately designed to allow each presenter to infuse their own personality into their presentation. In my case, while there are numerous ways to begin a presentation, I always select the one(s) that I am comfortable using, such as telling a story, using humour (not a joke), asking a question, getting the audience to do something, or stating the outcomes my audience can expect from the presentation. I stay away from starting with facts, statements and statistics. These may work very well for other presenters but I choose not to use them.

The template gives you a clear structure to follow and shows you the different ways to keep your audience engaged. As I said earlier, the idea with a presentation is to select the elements that will work for you. The idea is not to use all of them together and not to use ones with which you are uncomfortable. I might use two or three of these elements together (there might even be four, if one of the three chosen elements contains some humour), depending on the length of the presentation, but that is the most I am prepared to start with.

As you can see from the template, I have included a number of different roadmaps/structures that can be used in presentations. Ideally, I like to use a single structure in a presentation but sometimes this is not practical. Sometimes you might need a couple of different structures. In a single presentation a presenter might use a rhetorical question structure for most of the presentation but might include a numerical structure to support a point they are making. I once helped a client build a presentation using a rhetorical question structure but encouraged him to finish with a numerical structure. His closing listed the five benefits to doing business with his company. However, any more than two structures can cause confusion for your audience. Again, select the structures you are comfortable with (or that are insisted upon in certain environments). Using no more than two makes it easier for your audience to follow. (I have not listed all of the roadmaps on the template but have left space for you to add one in if you choose to use one that is not there already.)

You can see some of the ways I suggest closing a presentation in the template. Whenever possible, this closing will always follow the Q&A section of the presentation, if there is one. I know that sometimes a conference is set up so that you must answer questions at the end of the presentation, but try to avoid it where possible. The words a presenter leaves their audience with are often the ones they remember the most, so leave them with something you would want them to remember.

Finally, there is a list of the audience engagement elements in the template. Again I always select the ones I am comfortable with, enjoy using or feel are appropriate for the audience to which I am speaking. I will weave these elements through my entire presentation to ensure that I bring my audience on the journey with me.

The way to use the template is to start by answering the two questions in the pre-presentation section. Write your answers onto the template. Next, brainstorm every idea that could potentially be used in your presentation on a flip chart, white board, with Post-it notes or in a notebook. (If asked to give a presentation at short notice, you can even brainstorm on the reverse side of the template.) By doing this you create a pool of information and ideas from which to draw the most suitable content.

The next step is to decide on the message you want to get across and the key points you want to use to support that message. Again write this onto the template. After that draw a circle on the template around each element you are going to use in each of the remaining sections. For example, if you are going to open with a question, put a circle around 'A Question'. If you are going to close with a call to action, put a circle around 'Call to Action'. Also circle each of the audience engagement elements you intend to use. Once you have done this you have a physical guide that you can refer back to as you are crafting your presentation.

Not only will you become a better presenter by applying the thinking behind the TRUE presentation template, you will also be able to create and deliver better presentations in a shorter period of time. For many presenters, the elements I suggest using will take a little bit of getting used to, simply because of where and when in the presentation I am suggesting they be used. Like anything new or different, the key is practice. Get comfortable with this new approach to presenting and the improvements will be plentiful.

There are two ways to practise getting comfortable with a presentation. The first is by running through the presentation in advance in its entirety. Personally, I find this difficult. If I am preparing for a presentation that is fifteen minutes or longer I find that I don't always have long enough windows in which to practise. The second way to practise is to work on a couple of sentences or a couple of minutes of your presentation at a time. I find this works much more effectively for me. I can practise a sentence or two, or a paragraph, or a couple of minutes worth any time I am alone throughout the day. I might only have a five-minute window, but this is ample time to practise a selected part of my presentation. Throughout the day I may find a number of five-to-ten-minute windows that will allow me to complete practising my presentation in full. That said, all presenters are different, so find the way that works for you.

You will notice that so far I have made no reference to how you deliver the presentation. At this point you should be focused on creating a presentation that reinforces the message you want to get across. There is no point in having great delivery if your message isn't clear and no one knows what you want them to do at the end of your presentation.

Once you have a presentation you are sure will do the job, my suggestion for delivery is as follows:

1. Recognise that delivering a presentation requires a set of physical skills (such as voice, eye contact, how a presenter moves, pausing) to ensure that your body language and gestures support your message and are not a distraction. So study the skills in Chapter 10 and practise getting comfortable applying them.

2. Record your practice sessions every time, either by videoing them or recording yourself on an audio device. Video works best because you can see and hear how you are presenting. That said there are times when I will deliberately record with an audio device only. I do this because it allows me to focus only on what I am saying and how I am saying it, and not become distracted by watching my movement, body language and gestures. Equally, there will be occasions when I will watch a video practice session (or a live presentation) with the sound on mute so that I can focus on my movement, body language and gestures without being distracted by the words. When you play back a recording you will identify what you do well and what could be improved upon. You will also be your own biggest critic and supporter, and be keener than anyone else to make the necessary improvements.

CHOOSING YOUR ELEMENTS

TRUE criteria (set your own presentation score)

The objective of the TRUE presentation template is to encourage presenters to create presentations that will resonate with their audience and deliver a clear compelling message that is easy to understand.

The template will help you because you can use it to identify the elements that will allow you to create a presentation that has the highest score possible. Use the TRUE template to identify the elements you would like to include in your presentation and then use the TRUE Presentation Scorecard to identify the score that each of these elements achieves. This will give you a starting point from which to work. You can set this as your minimum requirement. The higher the score the better – just don't use every element in each section. I did have one presenter who tried to use all the positive score elements that are found in the presentation opening. If you try to do this, rather than helping you may find you are actually making things more difficult for yourself. As you become more familiar with the scorecard, you can use it to set higher scores for which to aim, if that is what you wish to do.

However, in many ways, setting a higher score each time is irrelevant. The key measure of success is to compare the score your presentation generates using positive score elements with a presentation you may have given or sat through that has included some of the negative score elements. The difference in scores will be noticeable, as will be the audience's engagement.

Think back to the example I gave early in this book. One group of presenters who were delivering an average of 100 presentations a year each scored -320 on the scorecard because they were using many of the negative score elements that so many presenters use in corporate and business presentations. Once they had removed the negative score elements and replaced them with positive score elements their score rose to +590 and their sales increased by fifteen per cent over the next three months.

In order to demonstrate clearly how to use the scorecard

and template effectively, I will now show you how I used it to create a high-scoring presentation that I delivered to an audience of approximately 150 sales professionals.

The pre-presentation phase

Personally, I find the pre-presentation phase to be the most important part of the presentation. It allows me to bring real clarity to what I need to say and helps me to make it relevant to my audience. For the pre-presentation phase I completed the three elements on the TRUE template.

1. I asked, 'Who is my audience?' (+40 pts)

My audience for this specific presentation was made up of sales professionals, sales managers, sales directors and some business owners. The audience was a mix of both women and men with a 35–65 per cent split. They varied in age from early twenties to late fifties/early sixties. They worked for large corporations, small-to-medium enterprises and were self-employed. The common denominator was that they were interested in improving their sales performance. Knowing this allowed me to include sales-related stories that I believed would resonate because they relayed experiences that this audience could identify with.

2. I asked, 'What is my objective?' (+40 pts)

My objective was to persuade them that I could help them create and deliver sales presentations that would be more persuasive and engaging than they were currently delivering.

My objective was to have one or more members of the audience invite me to help them improve an existing presentation.

3.   Brainstorming (+40 pts)

In spite of being very familiar with the content for this presentation, I always brainstorm in the pre-presentation phase. It eliminates complacency and keeps me focused on making sure I do my best for my audience. In this case the brainstorming was conducted alone. I brainstormed for about four days, giving an hour here and there throughout those four days. In total, I spent approximately five hours thinking about content that could potentially go into the presentation. I set up a flip chart in my office and put any ideas I came up with during the four days onto Post-it notes (one per note) and stuck them onto the flip chart. I filled up a couple of pages with ideas. I also carried a notebook around with me and put ideas into it as they came to me. In the end I had about sixty ideas from which to select the material that was most suitable for this audience and this objective. The ideas that came to me included the content I wanted to cover, the stories I could use to reinforce the points I wanted to make, and the different techniques I could use to keep my audience engaged throughout.

Overleaf are some of the ideas I came up with for the presentation I was delivering to this group of sales professionals:

Note that at this point I was not looking to construct the presentation, nor looking to place the content, and certainly not thinking about PowerPoint slides (I hadn't even decided if I was going to use slides).

My score for the pre-presentation phase was +120 points. The actions of answering the two questions and gathering up as much information as possible before I began constructing my presentation gave me the best chance to create a presentation that met the four TRUE criteria.

Presentation message

The next part of the presentation that I looked at was choosing the message I wanted to get across. My message had to be relevant to the audience. It had to be a single and clear message. In this case my message was: 'Using the TRUE presentation principles can help you create presentations that engage audiences, deliver compelling messages and help you win more business.'

Once I had identified this I had a **single message (+40 pts)** and a **clear message (+40 pts)**. This did two things for me. First, it made it easier to select content from my brainstorming session that would best support the message. Second, it made it easier to create a presentation that was understandable. **My score for the presentation message phase was +80 points** and I was comfortable that my chosen message would contribute to meeting the TRUE criteria.

Presentation structure

The next thing I did was select the presentation roadmaps that I was going to use. Sometimes I do this based on the structures I like using. My personal favourite is the 'rhetorical question structure' and I aim to use this as often as possible. In this case, however, I decided to use a **compare and contrast (+30)** structure. The content I chose to include in the presentation was influenced by the objective of the presentation and the message I wanted to get across. I wanted to set out elements that hinder many presenters in getting their message across during presentations, such as a poor opening or having too many messages, and contrast that with approaches that would improve the impact and effectiveness of their presentation. I did not speak about every element. The ones I chose to speak about were the ones that allowed me to connect most effectively with the audience. I also wanted to illustrate the importance of having one clear message, regardless of the length of a presentation, and suggest a number of ways to begin a presentation that would capture the audience's attention.

I also decided to use a **modular (+30)** structure, dividing this presentation into three stand-alone parts. The first module was aimed at getting the audience to acknowledge that the quality of presentations can vary from the very good – those which are engaging, draw the audience in and capture their attention – to the very bad, which are dull, lifeless, boring and cause audiences and prospective clients to stop listening.

The second module would highlight some of the elements that presenters use that cause audiences to lose interest and stop listening, such as the overuse of industry jargon or content that is too technical. My aim was to get my audience to acknowledge that they used some of these elements. I would then give examples of elements that could be used to capture an audience's attention and keep them engaged, such as audience involvement. During this presentation I would ask my audience to physically do something on a number of occasions.

The third module explained the TRUE presentation principles, template and scorecard. The 'positive score elements' and 'negative score elements' would be explained and supported with examples that illustrated how the audience could benefit from making changes to their presentations.

My score for the presentation structure phase is +60 points. The two structures I chose met three of the four TRUE criteria, in that they contributed to the audience's thinking, aided recall and made the presentation easy to follow and understand.

The presentation opening

The next thing I did was decide how to open my presentation. My aim was to disrupt my audience's thinking. To get them to stop thinking about everything else and instead focus on my presentation. So I started by asking them **three questions (+20 pts for each)**. Question number one was 'Have you ever sat through a presentation that was dull, boring and lifeless?' Question number two was 'Have you ever sat through a presentation that captured your attention from the word go and held it throughout?' Question number three was 'What was the difference between the two?' For questions one and two they answered by raising their hands and for question three they answered by calling out the reasons they believed one presentation was very good and the other very poor.

I also **stated my outcomes (+40 pts)** and then I **referenced something mentioned earlier (+10 pts)**. One of the presenters who had spoken before me (who was female and attractive) had started their presentation by saying, 'I'm turned on.' It was a deliberate play on words. She was testing to see if her microphone was working properly and that she could be heard clearly. It generated a reaction because of the double entendre. I started my presentation with the very same words, which generated laughter because it was a reference to something they had heard earlier. I then reinforced the laughter by having a bit of fun at my own expense, saying 'Funny how those words don't have the same effect when said by a bald man in his fifties.' This generated more laughter and added **humour (+30 pts)** to my opening.

My score for the presentation opening phase was +140 points – the combination of these different elements definitely disrupted my audience's thinking and, when combined, met the four TRUE criteria.

The presentation closing

Next I decided how I was going to close my presentation. My aim was to reinforce the message I wanted my audience to take away. I wanted them to hear something that made them think that they should be applying TRUE presentation thinking to how they create and deliver presentations. My preferred option for closing a presentation is with a story that will drive home my message with a soft-sell approach, allowing my audience to reach their own conclusions. That said I will use the 'call to action' or a 'recap of the benefits' when appropriate.

For this presentation, I chose to finish as follows. First, I used a metaphor and compared giving presentations to day one at the US Masters golf tournament at Augusta. Let me explain. There is a golfing quote that says something along the lines of you can't win the Masters on the Thursday (day one), but you can lose it. Presentations are similar. Good presentations may not win you business, but poor presentations can lose you business. I used this metaphor to reinforce the idea that presenters should be preparing a presentation that gives them the best chance of winning business.

Second, given that I was looking to drive home the idea of TRUE presentations, I asked my audience if my presentation had (in their eyes and ears) met the four criteria. I asked them if it contributed to their **Thinking,** if it was delivered in a way that was easy to **Understand** and if it was **Engaging.** Regarding the fourth criteria, **Recall,** I decided to set the audience a challenge. I offered a free coaching session to the first person who contacted me via email a week later, stating something that they could remember from this presentation. (A week later I received six emails from people who attended the presentation, telling me what they could remember from it.)

The **metaphor (+40 pts)** helped to reinforce my message and contributed to my audience's thinking, aided understanding, recall and engagement. I then asked **three questions (+20 pts for each)** and finally finished with a **call to action (+30 pts). My score for the presentation closing phase is +130 points** and again, the combination of these different elements reinforced the message I wanted my audience to take away and contributed to the presentation meeting the four TRUE criteria.

Audience engagement

Finally, I decided how I wanted to keep my audience engaged

throughout my presentation. I included **stories (+40 pts)** and **humour (+30 pts)** throughout. I asked **questions (+20 pts)** (sometimes the question was a simple as 'Does that make sense?' purely to ensure that my audience was still listening). I made an **emotional connection (+40 pts)** (stories contributed to this) because I knew that emotional connection would be stronger than a logical connection. I got the audience to **do something (audience involvement, +30 pts)** – I asked members of the audience to do the tear the sheet of paper exercise I mentioned in Chapter 7. I brought three people up to the speaking area to **draw on a flip chart (audience involvement, +30 pts)**. I used an **acronym (R.E.M.) (rhetorical device, +10)** to illustrate a point and generate a reaction (in this case a groan) from the audience. I used the **flip chart (prop, +30)** myself to explain how I use these audience engagement elements to keep my audience engaged throughout my presentations.

In a forty-minute presentation like this, my aim is to include an audience engagement element at least every five minutes. For this presentation I deliberately included seven different audience engagements tools and used some of them a number of times (stories, humour, questions) regularly throughout. In total, there were fifteen occasions when I used these elements, giving me an audience engagement element every three minutes.

My score for the audience engagement phase is +230 points. The combination of these different elements went a long way towards keeping my audience engaged throughout and contributed to the presentation meeting the four TRUE criteria. (A number of attendees have been in touch since to say how much they enjoyed the presentation.)

One question I get asked on occasion is, 'Can I give myself plus marks for each time I use a positive score element?' For example, if a presenter delivers a presentation that has three or four stories in it, can they award plus points for each story? The answer is yes. For me, however, that is not the important consideration. The important consideration is recognising the impact that the stories and questions and other positive score elements have when compared to the negative score elements. **My total score for this presentation was +730 pts**.

NOTE

The objective of this presentation was to persuade the attendees that I could help them create and deliver sales presentations that would help them win more business. At the time of writing this, five months after delivering the presentation, six different organisations who attended that day have been in touch to discuss how I might be able to help them.

CONCLUSION:
NOW IT'S YOUR TURN

So there you have it. My take on what is required to create presentations that will engage audiences and get them to buy into your idea or message. Now it's your turn. What will you do?

I know from experience that the easy thing to do is to read about the ideas that can help, but the hard part is putting them into practice. I know it will be challenging to apply the principles of TRUE presentations to your future presentations. It will probably be a step outside your comfort zone. The temptation will be to stick with what you have used before, but I encourage you to give TRUE a try.

Here's what I suggest. Take it one step at a time. Don't try to change everything immediately. The opening and the closing are often the easiest to change. Attendees of my training often tell me, afterwards, that the first two changes they made were to no longer finish their presentations with the Q&A and to remove the slide that says 'Thank you'. They will replace these with a call to action or a story, and leave the message they want their audience to take away as the last words on the slide. These are simple but effective changes.

Equally, the opening can easily be changed from being presenter-focused to being a question, story or quotation, all aimed at disrupting the audience's attention. My view is that you can start with one of these straightforward changes, get comfortable with it, and then move on to the next change.

It is important to select the change that is easiest for you. Start or finish with a story, if you are comfortable telling stories. If you are comfortable using humour, then use humour.

Ensure you measure your presentation's score on the scorecard. What are you including in the presentation that is helping get your message across? What is hindering it? The benefit of this is that you become familiar with the positive score elements and aware of the negative elements that you are employing. The more practice you get, the higher your score will become.

Finally, let me know how you get on. I would love to hear your success stories. I am currently working with a client who has embraced the TRUE principles. She recently gave a short presentation where she decided to begin it by lying face-up on the stage in order to represent someone lying on a hospital operating theatre table. Did this capture her audience's attention? Did it pique their curiosity? Absolutely. Now I know what you're thinking: 'I can't do that in a business presentation', and yes, you're probably right. It's not about lying on the floor, however; it's about disrupting their thinking and standing out as being different.

So now it's your turn. Apply the principles of TRUE presentations. Look to add the positive score elements that will help you get your message across and remove the negative score elements. For a copy of the complete Presentation Scorecard go to www.arkspeakingandtraining.com/contact-us and fill in the contact form. I wish you every success with your future presentations.

SUGGESTED FURTHER READING

Antion, Tom, *Wake 'Em Up! How to Use Humor & Other Professional Techniques to Create Alarmingly Good Business Presentations* (Anchor Publications, Landover Hills, 1997)

Brown, Mark, Fripp, Patricia, LaCroix, Darren, Tate, E. and Valentine, C., *Speaker's Edge: Secrets and Strategies for Connecting with any Audience* (Soar with Eagles, Arkansas, 2010)

Carnegie, Dan, *How to Develop Self-Confidence & Influence People by Public Speaking* (Simon & Schuster, New York, 1991)

Davies, Graham, *The Presentation Coach: Bare Knuckle Brilliance for Every Presenter* (Capstone, Chichester, 2010)

Denning, Stephen, *The Leader's Guide to Storytelling: Master the Art and Discipline of Business Narrative* (Jossey-Bass, San Francisco, 2011)

Dietz, Karen and Silverman, Lori L., *Business Storytelling for Dummies* (For Dummies, New Jersey, 2013)

Du Toit, Paul and Stevens, Alan, *The Exceptional Speaker: How to Deliver Sensational Speeches* (Congruence Press, Rivonia, 2013)

Duarte, Nancy, *slide:ology: The Art and Science of Creating Great Presentations* (O'Reilly Media, Boston, 2008)

Duarte, Nancy, *Resonate: Present Visual Stories That Transform Audiences* (John Wiley & Sons, New Jersey, 2010)

Garavan, T. N., Hogan, C. and Cahir-Donnell, A., *Making Training & Development Work: A Best Practice Guide* (Oak Tree Press, Dublin, 2003)

Haven, Kendall, *Story Proof: The Science Behind the Startling Power of Story* (Libraries Unlimited, Santa Barbara, 2007)

Heath, Chip and Heath, Dan, *Made to Stick: Why Some Ideas Survive and Others Die* (Random House, New York, 2007)

Jackson, Lee, *PowerPoint Surgery: How to Create Presentation Slides that Make Your Message Stick* (Engaging Books, Leeds, 2013)

Ledden, Emma, *The Presentation Book: How To Create It, Shape It and Deliver It! Improve Your Presentation Skills Now* (FT Press, New Jersey, 2014)

McKee, Robert, *Story: Substance, Structure, Style and the Principles of Screenwriting* (Methuen Publishing Ltd, London, 1999)

Reynolds, Garr, *Presentation Zen Design: Simple Design Principles and Techniques to Enhance Your Presentation* (New Riders, San Francisco, 2009)

Reynolds, Garr, *Presentation Zen: Simple Ideas on Presentation Design and Delivery* (New Riders, San Francisco, 2011)

Simmons, Annette, *The Story Factor: Inspiration, Influence and Persuasion Through the Art of Storytelling* (Basic Books, New York, 2006)

Weissman, Jerry, *Presenting to Win: The Art of Telling Your Story* (FT Press, New Jersey, 2008)